THE TEACHER TALK ADVANTAGE

Five Voices of Effective Teaching

Chick Moorman and Thomas Haller

Personal Power Press
Merrill, Michigan

THE TEACHER TALK ADVANTAGE

Five Voices of Effective Teaching

©2012 by Chick Moorman, Thomas Haller and Personal
Power Press

Library of Congress Catalogue Card Number: 2011943230

ISBN 978-0-9821568-4-1

Printed in the United States of America

Personal Power Press
P.O. Box 547, Merrill, MI 48637

Cover Design
Zachary Parker, zdp431@gmail.com

TABLE OF CONTENTS

Introduction ....**xiii**

The Voice of Structure.. **1**

"Let me explain the morning routine."............................ 3

"Let's review the morning routine." 4

"It's time to begin.".. 5

"These are the rules for our classroom." 6

"In this classroom we observe healthy limits." 7

"Here are the Responsible Action Statements we
  live by in this classroom." 8

"Mistakes are permitted here." 9

"Your behavior equals a choice." 10

"Speak up for yourself." 11

"Every problem is an opportunity.".............................. 11

"Level of risk is your choice."....................................... 12

"Finding solutions is the focus.".................................... 13

"Charles, thank you for asking. That's a perfect
  example of one of our Responsible Action
  Statements: 'Speak up for yourself.'"............................ 13

"I've seen some behaviors that don't fit with
our Responsible Action Statements." 15

"Let's talk about rights and responsibilities." 16

"Please add this to your Responsibility Notebook." 17

"It's time for a lesson on put-downs." 18

"That's a put-down. We don't talk that way in
this classroom." 20

"Step on it." 21

"If you don't get this the first time, would that
be all right?" 23

"I did it on purpose to see if you would notice." 24

"Thanks for pointing that out." 25

"What a silly mistake that was." 26

"Let's stop a minute and see what we can learn
from that error." 26

"Get out your risk pads." 28

"Now stretch your answer even more." 29

"Let's see who can be first, best, fastest, do the
most." 29

"It's time for partner work." 31

"Everybody find a partner." 31

"Keep a straight face." 33

"Get out your blockers." 34

"It's time to activate our inside blockers." 35

"Keep your eyes on your own paper." 36

"If I see you looking at another's paper, yours
will go in the basket and you'll get a zero." 37

"Correct your own papers." 38

"Cathy, we need to have a talk about your
math papers." 39

"I'm going to use the name jar." 40

"Let's have a whip-around." 41

"No hands in the air. Only writing." 42

"Great answer." 43

"What is ONE way their goods can be shipped
   to market?" 45

"And what do you think about that, Miss Wilson?" 46

"That would be an interesting topic for another
   day." 47

"Let's give Ahmed the silent cheer." 48

"Let's revisit something we learned earlier
   this semester." 49

The Voice of Nurture 53

"Sometimes things happen." 55

"What an honor that he chose to land on you." 56

"I can see you boys are angry." 57

"Show me just how angry you are." 58

"You seem extremely frustrated." 59

"You can feel angry, and you don't get to call
   him names." 59

"Stop crying and listen to me." 60

"You seem sad." 61

"Help me understand what you're feeling." 62

"Your teeth are clenched and your hands are
   so tight your knuckles are turning white." 63

"I understand just how you feel." 64

"Alec, you seem upset." 64

"Don't be silly. It wasn't that bad." 65

"That's too bad." 66

"It'll be okay, honey. Lots of kids move." 67

"Equations can be very frustrating, can't they?" 68

"You should know by now that I'm not the
same as every other teacher." 69
"I'm sad that happened. If anyone can handle
it, you can." 70
"Oh, my. I see tears." 71
"It was an accident." 73
"Good morning, Esther." 74
"I noticed you were at the basketball game last
night." 75
"Thank you for sharing that, Charles." 77
"Kelly, give me a high-five." 77
"Estaban, will you help me with this?" 78
"I'm thinking about getting a dog. Do you think
a cocker spaniel would be good in an apartment?" 79
"Circle the names of the teachers you feel you had
a meaningful relationship with this year." 80
"I am Mr. Wilson and I teach government. I think
I know most of you, and I'm happy to have you
here in class." 82
"I'm enjoying the seriousness with which many
of you are taking this." 85
"All of you would like my attention right now." 86
"That wasn't such a good idea, was it?" 87

The Voice of Teaching **89**
"Get in your seats." 94
"I'm on page 61." 95
"How many colonies were there?" 96
"Come up with a question that asks for higher-
level thinking." 97
"What is *one* good reason why?" 99
"Who would be willing to read the paragraphs?" 100

"There will usually be four choices on a multiple-
   choice question. One or two of the answers you
   will know are not correct, so eliminate those
   and guess among the remaining options
   that seem possible to you." 101
"If you don't know the answer, make an educated
   guess." 103
"I think I'll get started correcting these papers. A
   fast start helps motivate me to keep going." 104
"I'm sorry." 105
"I am aware that I listed the wrong assignment on
   the web site. I see the confusion it created. I'm
   sorry. I will double-check the listings for
   accuracy from now on." 106
"I'm sorry that I reprimanded you in front of the
   class, but your choice of behavior was
   inappropriate." 106
"We have a problem." 107
"I'm concerned that . . ." 108
"I am not interested in blaming, only in finding
   a solution." 109
"Act as if you can." 111
"The words you use to talk to yourself are
   like seeds you plant in your mind." 113
"What did you tell yourself?" 115
"Write down all the negative comments you
   can think of about math." 116
"Now ball up your papers and crush them in
   your hands." 117
"Richard, that's an excuse. Excuses are not
   accepted in this classroom because . . ." 118

"We're going to learn another responsibility
  skill today." 121

"Time to get ready to go home." 123

"Are you on TOPIC?" 125

"OK, get back to your seats. Put the
  microscopes away. No more responsibility for
  you until you can show me you know how to
  be responsible." 126

"Let me show you how we put the microscopes
  away." 127

"Tell me what it looks like to . . ." 128

"Let me tell you what I noticed when you used
  microscopes yesterday." 129

"Help me collect what it looks like and sounds
  like." 130

"Help me plan the day tomorrow." 132

"How will we know if we've been successful?" 132

"What are you trying to accomplish?" 134

"Compare this paper to the one you did earlier." 134

"Do you see any growth?" 136

"What *will* you do?" 137

"Thank you for sharing your feelings with me." 138

"I'm feeling apprehensive about this." 139

"There is no such thing as luck." 140

"What do you attribute that to?" 142

"I just want you to do it to see if you can." 143

"Because it feels good on the inside when you
  accomplish something." 145

"If you read fifty books, you can have a pizza
  party." 146

"You did a good job on that." 148

"Marti is doing great work in spelling." 149

"Outstanding attitude." 150

"I'll be passing out the Good-Student Awards
   now." 152

"The statistics you included pointed the reader
   right to your conclusion." 153

"Bill, I noticed you ignored Carlos's teasing and
   immediately returned to work." 154

"Thank you for cleaning up the paint brushes
   before you left yesterday. You saved me fifteen
   minutes." 155

"Wow! That is unbelievable!" 156

The Voice of Debriefing **157**

"I'll be collecting your assignments now." 159

"Get with your interaction trio. We're going to
   debrief this experience." 160

"Let's talk about what happened at the
   assembly." 162

"Let me hear some of your reactions." 163

"Let's make a list." 164

"Notice how you react if that pounding starts
   again!" 165

How to Ignore a Distraction 166

"What evidence did you see that your classmates
   were ignoring distractions?" 167

"What did you do that was respectful?" 168

"What do you think would have happened
   if . . . ?" 169

"See if you can summarize in one sentence what you
   learned about owning your own behavior." 169

"Which one was the best, in your opinion? The
worst?"... 170

"How is the skill we learned today similar to
the one we learned yesterday?" 170

"What could you do to improve your score on
this?".. 171

"What pattern do you see about your own behavior
in regard to respecting others?"...................... 172

"Where else could you use this skill in your
life?" 172

"Turn to your partner and give each other a
high-five.".. 174

"What possibilities exist for . . . ?" 175

"Your behavior was inappropriate."........................ 175

"Hiam, let's talk about your plan." 176

"How is Jean Paul's plan working from your
point of view?" 177

"I've been hearing some nice things about
you." 178

"Let's look at some of the decisions you
made.".. 179

"Time for another 3-D lesson." 180

The Voice of Accountability **183**

"Opportunity equals responsibility." 185

"In this room you have an opportunity to sit by
a friend. Your responsibility is to stay on task
and refrain from engaging in side
conversations." 186

"It's up to you.".. 188

Choose, Decide, Pick 189

"If you choose to throw the blocks, you will be deciding to have a different activity this morning." 190

"If you choose to run in the hall, I will walk you to the bus for the next two days." 191

"If you decide to throw snowballs during recess, you are choosing to stand next to me." 192

"I see you have chosen to have me sign [not sign] your eligibility card." 194

"Just because I like you, do you think I should let you get away with it?" 195

"Putting other people down gets you one more page of writing sentences, Arwa." 196

"That's it. Give me your cell phone. You can get it back next week." 197

"Bend over and grab your ankles." 198

"You're asking for the paddle." 200

"Sounds to me like you don't want recess today." 201

"It's time to walk and think." 202

"You asked for it. Now you're going to get it." 205

Move Up Before You Move In 206

Talk to yourself before you talk to the student. 207

See it all as perfect 208

Honor that what is, is. 209

Make no assumptions. 209

"I have several questions to ask." 210

"Let's make a list of what we learned." 211

"It looks like a bunch of slobs ate in the lunchroom today." 212

"Looks like you made the wrong choice." 213

"Looks like you don't get it yet. I'll have to
increase the penalty."...214
"No, I'm not going to get you in trouble, but
you might."...215
"You just got a detention." 216
"I'm glad you're back from the Responsibility
Room."...217
"Hello, Mrs. Radison. Richie chose some behaviors
this morning that resulted in a Responsibility
Room assignment from Mr. Tanner.".......................219
"Nice to have you back. I missed your smile.
Tell me about your plan." 220
"So what surprised you about implementing
the plan?"..220
"I'm wondering what you're going to do for
restorative action."..222
"You asked for this punishment, so now you'll
have to deal with it."...223

Conclusion..**225**
About the Authors..**231**
Other Books and Products **235**
Training Opportunities......................................**239**

INTRODUCTION

Mrs. Brown taught fourth grade. She was able to get most of the students to do what she wanted most of the time. Her students acted respectfully and responsibly. They listened to directions and followed them. They enjoyed school and the positive relationships they created there. They achieved, academically and behaviorally.

The teacher across the hall also taught fourth grade. That's where the similarity ends. This teacher struggled to get students to do what she wanted. Their behaviors were often disrespectful and they frequently assumed the victim stance. They ignored directions even when they heard them. Many of these students didn't like school much. Their academic and behavioral achievement suffered.

Both teachers were veteran educators. Both loved teaching. Both desired the same results: respectful, responsible students who achieved and behaved. One was able to get those results. The other was not. What was the difference? Verbal skills. One teacher had effective verbal skills. The other did not.

The Teacher Talk Advantage is jam-packed with verbal skills that will help you create the classroom you desire. These skills will help you become the professional educator you always wanted to be. They will reduce your stress and help you motivate and inspire your students.

The skills in this book are divided into five chapters representing five voices: The Voice of Structure, The Voice of Nurture, The Voice of Teaching, The Voice of Debriefing, and the Voice of Accountability. These are the five essential voices that are necessary for teaching effectively in today's world. If you *work* these skills, they will *work* for you to help you create your grandest vision of an exceptional classroom, one that is both emotionally and intellectually healthy for all concerned.

Most of the names in this book are fictitious. Some are not. All of the events and examples are real, drawn from incidents we have witnessed in classrooms or heard about in workshops or counseling sessions. They are real stories of real people working with real students in real schools. On occasion we have combined more than one event or story into one concise example.

Thank you to all who have sent us ideas and encouragement as we worked on this manuscript. Thank you to those who have attended our workshops, asked challenging questions, spewed out your frustration, or shared your success stories. Thank you for your e-mails and responses to our newsletters and blogs. Your input has been invaluable.

Thank you for holding this book in your hands. Thank you for reading it. Thank you for implementing the ideas you will find here.

Thank you for passing it on.

THE VOICE OF STRUCTURE

The voice of structure is about setting a routine and sticking to it. It involves ritual and order. Routine and order are important to the human brain. When there is stability in the classroom, a student can predict what is coming next. When what comes next is evident, anxiety decreases and brain energy can be invested in learning and behavior management instead of in busily managing the flight or fight response.

Many students come from homes that do not have the type of order that makes classrooms run effectively. These students are not accustomed to the rituals and routines that are common in institutions of learning. When they know what to expect they are more likely to feel stable and are more able to handle the chaos that constantly swirls about them in today's world.

Some teachers call these routines "rules." Others refer to them as "norms" or "Responsible Action Statements." Regardless of what they are called, without rituals, routines, and agreed-upon expectations, students are often confused and left without the direction and support they need for stability.

The voice of structure is also about building a positive emotional climate in the classroom, one that students can expect and rely on. One of the correlates of the effective schools research from years past is a safe and orderly environment. This refers not only to physical safety, although that is certainly essential, but to emotional safety. Creating an appropriate structure in schools and classrooms is about providing a place where students feel safe to take risks and make mistakes and learn to both give and get respect.

A third part of the voice of structure requires creating a classroom arrangement that takes into account both the teacher's and the students' needs for power, autonomy, and relationship. Here we are talking about classroom control, a style of classroom management that finds an appropriate balance between teacher control and student control. We call this the democratic style of management—shared control. In this environment, students find a structure where they can experience security and freedom simultaneously.

The type and amount of control, structure, and security that exists within the classroom at any given moment is a product of the teacher's having created it through an abundance (or lack) of the skills necessary to implement effective management techniques. This section is designed to give you the verbal skills necessary to successfully create the classroom structure you desire.

> **"Let me explain the morning routine."**

Do you have classroom routines? Do you begin each day, each class period the same way? If not, you might want to consider developing a routine and sticking to it. It matters *less* what specific routine you use and *more* that you have one.

In one middle school class we know, the students come in, take their seats, look up at the board for a starter assignment, and begin working on it before the teacher even addresses the class. The procedure was taught, practiced and debriefed for several days before it became an unconscious action on the part of the students. Now the students simply do it. It has become routine.

Another teacher we observed has a procedure for students to follow when they return to school following an absence. They go to the teacher first thing in the morning (the teacher does not go to them), say "Hello," ask for a list of missing assignments, and say, "Thank you." They then return to their seats. Other students know the drill and work on their own material while the teacher responds to a returning student. It's all part of the routine. They have practiced it. They expect it. And they accept it.

"Let's review the morning routine."

Just because you have a routine doesn't mean that all students will follow it all the time. Yet, if you have a prevailing structure that includes specific ways things are done at specific times, you will experience less resistance, less reluctance, and less conflict.

Of course you will need to occasionally review the routines for how to start the day and what to do when the fire alarm goes off, the procedure to follow when a guest shows up in your classroom, how to leave the lunch table when you're finished eating, and what to do when you get a paper back from the teacher. Teaching, reviewing, debriefing, and reviewing again are all important in establishing meaningful routines that work.

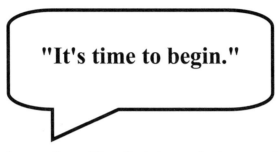

"It's time to begin."

Begin on time. The first two minutes are the most important minutes of each day and of each class period. This is where you communicate your commitment to the structure. This is where you demonstrate you will be following the established routine. This is where you begin modeling your seriousness, promptness, empathy, and sense of humor. Be aware that you are setting the tone for the entire day with your attitude and actions in the first two minutes.

Likewise, the first two weeks of each semester are the most important weeks. Here the routine is set—or not. Here rituals are created and followed—or not. This is when students learn whether you return papers on time or not, whether you have a positive attitude or not, and whether you can laugh or not.

New teachers are often advised, "Don't smile for the first month. You can always ease up later." Wrong. If you don't smile for the first month and then begin smiling, your students have already learned that you don't smile much and they won't trust that your smiling now is genuine. In the first month you are setting the tone for the entire semester. Are you doing that consciously and intentionally?

"These are the rules for our classroom."

Rules can help establish a routine. They also encourage resistance. Children love to break rules. For many of them, breaking the rules is fun and can even become their own personal ritual.

When you alone make up rules for your classroom, there is no buy-in on the part of the students. There is no ownership or understanding of the need for the rules. Many teachers present rules unaccompanied by reasons or student input. If students follow rules imposed under these circumstances, it's often the result of a state of being called "obedience." Obedience occupies the spot where internal ethics would be appropriate, and effectively prevents children from thinking and developing a positive internal standard of conduct.

More effective than rules are classroom norms, Responsible Action Statements, or healthy limits.

> **"In this classroom we observe healthy limits."**

We recently observed on the wall of a third-grade classroom the following rules:

- No running in the halls or classroom.
- No teasing.
- No hitting, pushing, or shoving.
- No snowball throwing on the playground.

By negatively phrasing her rules, this teacher helped create pictures in her students' minds of what she did *not* want. What she wanted was walking in the hall and classroom, yet her words did not produce that mental image in the minds of her students. Nor did they teach her students the behavior she desired. Her language patterns produced the opposite mental picture of what she really wanted.

Simply changing these negatively phrased statements to the desired behavior, stated positively, would help.

- Walk in the halls and classroom.
- Say kind words to one another.
- Touch others with their permission only.
- Allow snow to stay on the ground.

To strengthen these norms even further, this teacher could consider reframing them as "healthy limits." Healthy limits are not rules. They are behavioral limits we observe in this environment for health and safety reasons.

We walk because it is safer for all of us. When snow is allowed to stay on the ground, there are fewer injuries and arguments. Saying nice things to each other reduces the incidence of emotional injuries. When you get permission before touching another person, fewer fights, injuries, and bad feelings manifest.

Having healthy reasons behind the limits gives them credibility. It is easy to resist or break a rule when it's just a rule. It's more difficult to choose a behavior that violates a healthy limit because there is awareness of the safety or health reason supporting it. We follow healthy limits not because they are rules. We follow them because they are healthy and for the benefit of all who enter the space.

> **"Here are the Responsible Action Statements we live by in this classroom."**

If your goal is to manage your classroom in a way that promotes self-responsibility, self-discipline, and self-motivation, consider using the following Responsible Action Statements or ones like them. These are basic tenets of how self-responsible people behave. Since self-responsible people are adept at taking care of themselves, we used the acronym **MYSELF** to help students remember them.

Mistakes are permitted here.

Your behavior equals a choice.

Speak up for yourself.

Every problem is an opportunity.

Level of risk is your choice.

Finding solutions is the focus.

Put these Responsible Action Statements on display so students can see them. Having them visible will also serve to remind you that these norms exist and need to be followed. Let's take a closer look at each one.

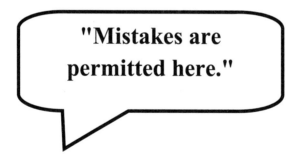

Having this statement on your Responsible Action Statements chart and repeating it throughout the year tells students clearly that part of the prevailing structure in this classroom is permission to make mistakes.

Students often see a mistake as something negative. A mistake in many classrooms is likely to get red-penciled, pointed out, and sometimes brought to public attention.

Mistakes are not bad. They are not awful. They are simply data that can be used to grow and evolve in uplifting and exciting ways. Mistakes are learning opportunities, a time to make amends, a chance to improve and do it differently next time. Making mistakes can be a powerful way to learn. "Mistakes are permitted here" tells students clearly that making a mistake is no measure of their self-worth or of their character.

> ## "Your behavior equals a choice."

Students are making choices in your classroom every day. They choose to turn their papers in on time or not. They choose to volunteer an answer or not. They choose to do their paper on Balboa or Cartier. They choose to follow the Responsible Action Statements or not. They choose to handwrite their paper or use the computer. Even making no choice is a choice.

Students also choose their behaviors. They choose whether to be interested or bored, happy or frustrated, distracting, distracted, or attentive.

This Responsible Action Statement is designed to help students take responsibility for the fact that they are always in the process of choosing—whether they are conscious of it or not.

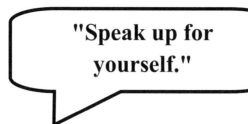

There are no mind readers in your classroom. You are most likely not a psychic and neither are your students. This is why students need to learn to speak up for themselves.

If they don't understand something, they need to say so. If they are unclear about something and sit on their hands without speaking up, they are not taking full responsibility for their learning. If someone in their group is not doing what is important, they need to tell them. If there is a problem on the bus or playground, they need to tell you.

If they don't speak up for themselves, who will? Help them take another step toward self-responsibility by making *speak up for yourself* an integral piece of your classroom structure.

"Every problem is an opportunity."

Everyone has problems. Every classroom, every school, and every teacher has problems. New problems spring from solutions to previous problems. We never totally get rid of problems.

It is important to help students see problems as positive, as opportunities to grow and learn. Problems give us data about both what we know and what we need to learn. Problems encourage us to engage in the search for solutions, and that is what self-responsible people do.

> ## "Level of risk is your choice."

What is involved in taking a risk? It means taking action even though you might fail. It's moving ahead even though you're a bit fearful.

Feeling fearful is not a reason to not do something. Some risks are worth taking. As a result of taking worthwhile risks, your students can learn more and do more.

We are not talking about foolish risks here. This is not about driving 100 miles an hour or playing in the street. It's not about trying drugs or experimenting with sex. This is about taking the risk of picking a challenging subject for your science project. It's about deciding how much to share when you tell a personal story. It involves choosing to read and report on a type of book you have never chosen before.

If you use this Responsible Action Statement as part of your classroom structure and help students see that it makes sense, they will risk more and learn more.

"Finding solutions is the focus."

Would you rather have the emphasis in your classroom be on fixing blame or fixing problems? This tenet is designed to create a solution-seeking mindset for you and your students in which the emphasis is on problem solving, not finding and punishing people who are at fault.

Consider fault to be an F-word in your classroom. Refuse to use it. Instead of talking about fault, talk about the R-word: responsibility.

"Charles, thank you for asking. That's a perfect example of one of our Responsible Action Statements: 'Speak up for yourself.'"

"Did you all hear what Charles just did? He didn't understand why one-third is bigger than one-fourth so he asked about it. That's what we call taking responsibility for yourself by speaking up. Way to go, Charles."

"OK, so there seems to be a problem staying focused when the construction workers are making noise in the room next door. This problem gives us the opportunity to find a solution and put one of our Responsible Action Statements to work for us. Can anybody tell me which one?"

"Carlotta, thank you for saying 'I pass' on this. That shows you trust our Responsible Action Statement 'Level of risk is your choice.' Yes, you get to decide how much you risk, if anything, as we share these with each other."

Each of the Teacher Talk examples above was spoken by a teacher who is breathing life into the Responsible Action Statements in his or her classroom. These important statements have to be more than mere phrases posted on the wall. Students won't even know what some of these words and phrases mean until you show concrete examples of them in action. Responsible Action Statements refer to actions. Unless people are acting on them, they are empty sayings.

Point out examples of these statements being acted on, live by them, model them, and apply these concepts to the situations that naturally arise during the year. Make them come alive in your classroom.

> **"I've seen some behaviors that don't fit with our Responsible Action Statements."**

Yes, mention those incidents where you see examples of students choosing behaviors that violate the Responsible Action Statements.

- "I'm hearing some of you being upset with your speed of learning Spanish. Remember, mistakes are permitted here."
- "Today I heard someone say, 'He made me do it.' In our classroom, your behavior equals a choice."
- "I noticed some of you were upset with playing dodgeball again in physical education class. How would it change your perception of the class if you chose the responsible action of finding solutions rather than complaining about the teacher?"

Once again it is up to you to structure the ongoing practices in your classroom to fit with the Responsible Action Statements. That means living by the concepts, thus making them more than an attractive wall decoration.

> ## "Let's talk about rights and responsibilities."

Another way you could choose to provide ritual and structure for your classroom is to design that structure around the concepts of rights and responsibilities. The following sign was displayed in all classrooms in a Michigan middle school we visited.

1. I have the RIGHT to be safe;
   a. therefore,
   b. I have the RESPONSIBILITY to act peacefully, play safely, and to avoid threatening, teasing, or hurting others.
2. I have the RIGHT to learn;
   a. therefore,
   b. I have the RESPONSIBILITY to be on time for class, listen attentively, and to work and move about the school without disturbing others.
3. I have the RIGHT to be respected;
   a. therefore,
   b. I have the RESPONSIBILITY to respect the property of others and accept their right to privacy.

Everyone in the classroom has rights that need to be respected, and for every right there are responsibilities that go with it that respect the rights of others. This is civics in action. Rights and responsibilities are the cornerstone of a civilized society. A helpful place to have this important civics lesson come to life could be your classroom.

> ## "Please add this to your Responsibility Notebook."

Some schools have students use a planner where they keep track of assignments and have a parent sign it every night signifying that he or she has looked at it. Perhaps you have students write in a language arts journal that serves as a permanent record of their musings and your responses. Maybe you require students to keep a science or history notebook where they organize their notes, previous tests, and upcoming assignments. All are teaching methods designed to provide students with a system to keep track of their materials, important dates, and results.

So why not use a Responsibility Notebook? This could be a place where students keep their Responsible Action Statements, rights and responsibilities, or norms, depending on what you choose to call them. This is where they could make journal entries about responsibility issues that arise in your classroom.

If you teach your students five things they can do to ignore distractions, that list can go in the Responsibility Notebook. Four ways to respect the guest speaker can go there also. When you teach any responsibility behavior, such as how to disagree politely, get assignments if you have been absent, or speak up for yourself politely, it can go in this important notebook.

Just the fact of having a Responsibility Notebook sends an important message to students: responsibility is so important here that we even have a special notebook to keep track of it. Is it important enough in your classroom to have one? You get to decide.

> ## "It's time for a lesson on put-downs."

John Ash teaches eighth-grade social studies in a Michigan public school. His students are similar to other students around the country. They talk about clothes, video games, and the opposite sex. They also put each other down. "Klutz," "homo," and "retard" are a few of the more popular words they use to ridicule one another.

Tired of battling the verbal violence and wanting to create a structure that created a safe emotional environment, John recently created a plan to eliminate put-downs in his classroom. In each of his six classes, he taught his students about put-downs. He instructed them to take notes as he placed a definition of "put-down" on the board. He lectured about what put-downs were and what they were not. He shared and solicited examples of put-downs. He led a discussion on what it felt like to both send and receive them.

John then passed out a handful of paper slips to each student. He instructed them to use the slips to write put-downs about classmates, about themselves, and even about him. He assured them that these put-downs would be anonymous and would never be seen by anyone. He also explained that this was their last chance to get put-downs out of their systems because, beginning the next day, verbal violence would no longer be allowed in the classroom. He allowed five minutes of writing time, then collected the slips in a large paper grocery sack.

Students watched as their teacher stapled the bag shut. He then led them out the door, down the hall, and outside to where the cooks emptied the garbage. With his students standing in a circle, he held the bag of put-downs over a burn barrel and set it on fire. Students watched as their put-downs went up in smoke, a symbolic gesture that signaled the end of put-downs.

After everyone returned to the classroom, John told his students they had just witnessed a Viking funeral. Since the put-downs were now dead, he explained, they would no longer make an appearance in the classroom.

> **"That's a put-down. We don't talk that way in this classroom."**

The Viking funeral helped reduce put-downs among John Ash's eighth graders. It did not eliminate them. So in the days that followed, he employed a Teacher Talk skill designed to reduce put-downs even further. When he heard a put-down, he called it by name.

"That's a put-down," he would say. "We don't use put-downs in eighth grade because people can end up feeling hurt and it can lead to physical violence. What we do here is tell the other person how we feel and what we want to have happen. Please use that pattern when speaking to the person you're tempted to put down. What do you really want to tell that person?"

Without exception, John responded to put-downs identically: "That's a put-down. We don't use put-downs in eighth grade because people can end up feeling hurt and it can lead to physical violence. What we do here is tell the other person how we are feeling and what we want to have happen."

In less than a month, John drastically reduced the incidence of verbal violence in his classroom. Instead of "Hey, retard, you belong in Mrs. Olson's room with the other retards!" he had his students saying, "I'd appreciate it if you didn't bump my desk on the way to the pencil sharpener. It's irritating and I'd like it if you were more careful." "Knock it off, dog breath" was replaced by "I don't like it when you put your feet on my chair."

This activity obviously took a major commitment of time and effort on John's part to affect student behavior in this area—time taken away from the social studies curriculum. Why was he willing to do it? When asked, he responded, "I don't allow students to beat one another up with their fists, and I'm not going to let them do it with their words either. If I don't provide a structured environment where students feel safe emotionally, how much learning do you think will occur?"

John Ash still teaches eighth grade. His students still talk about clothes, video games, and the opposite sex, but they no longer put one another down. Instead, they have learned to communicate honestly and openly. They risk saying what they really mean. They can afford to take risks because they feel safe. After all, they are learning in a safe, orderly, and skillfully structured environment.

In a northern New York high school, twenty-four art students sat waiting for the teacher to begin the first day of instruction in drawing class. The teacher introduced himself and briefly told the students what they could expect during the semester. With the expectations clearly communicated, he then did the unexpected.

The art educator passed out a blank sheet of drawing paper to all the students. Pencils ready, they waited to receive their first assignment. They were in for a surprise. "Stand up, please," the teacher instructed. The students complied. "Now, put your paper on the floor in front of you," he continued. There was more than one quizzical look from his students as they slowly followed his directions.

When all students were standing with a blank paper on the floor in front of them, the teacher continued with his instructions. "Now step on it," he said. More puzzled looks followed. "I mean it," he continued. "Step on it. I want you to walk on your paper. In fact, I want you to stomp on it. Jump on it if you want to."

Some students eagerly complied. Others were hesitant. Eventually, all the students stepped on their papers, leaving shoe marks of various sizes and shapes on their previously clean sheets.

"Now turn the paper over," the teacher said, "and do the same on the other side. Leave some marks." The students did as instructed, not fully understanding what was going on. If nothing else, this teacher now had everyone's attention.

"Sit back down now," he said, when students had successfully scuffed up both sides of their papers. "Now draw on it. And whatever you do, don't throw it away. I want you to make something out of it."

Many students were uncertain about the directions and hesitated to add pencil to the papers with shoe marks on them. The teacher explained, "You are going to make some mistakes this semester. You might even think you have ruined some things. Mistakes can be used to make beautiful creations. Do not start over. Work with your mistakes. Make something beautiful out of your messes.

"Some of your best art can come from your mistakes. See those mistakes as opportunities to create something different. If somebody walks on your paper, use that to create art. If you slip and make something the wrong color, turn it into the right color by making an original creation out of it.

"Now, let's get to drawing." With that, this teacher clapped his hands twice and said, "Come on, let's see what you can do. Step on it."

> **"If you don't get this the first time, would that be all right?"**

"You don't have to learn everything today. Can anyone tell me why?"

"When you take this quiz in a moment, would it be OK if you missed some right answers? Why is that?"

These Teacher Talk examples fall into a category of verbal responses called *cushioning*. Cushioning is an attempt to reduce anxiety, decrease pressure, and free students up to relax into an activity so they can gain maximum benefit from it.

To put cushioning Teacher Talk into practice with your students, follow these two steps.

One: Make an assertion.

Two: Ask why.

"We don't always learn everything the first time." (assertion) "Why is that so?" (ask why)

Students might respond by telling you that it takes several repetitions before skills become natural, that they have to hear it two or three times before it sticks, or that sometimes they forget things and have to relearn a concept. Cushioning gives students permission to not have to learn everything this time, in this moment, right now. By giving them verbal permission to learn at their own pace, in accordance with their own time clock, you cushion the pressure to learn NOW and actually increase the chance that learning occurs in this moment.

It would be OK if you had to read this twice to understand it, wouldn't it? How come?

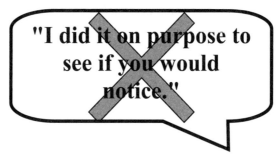

A first-year high school teacher made a spelling error on the board during the first week of school. As often happens in these kinds of situations, a well-intentioned student politely pointed out the mistake.

The rookie educator probably didn't realize that this event was a defining moment for him in terms of modeling the structure and prevailing atmosphere in his classroom.

How he handled this important situation would set the tone for the rest of the school year.

Wanting to look good in the eyes of his students, he replied, "I did it on purpose to see if you were paying attention." Some students believed him. Most did not. To our way of thinking, this claim should never be used when explaining a mistake unless it's true. And if it is true, why would you want to do that? Wouldn't it be a wiser use of your time to teach students the correct way to do something rather than seeing if you can catch them not paying attention? That strategy seems like a setup to us.

> ## "Thanks for pointing that out."

A third-grade teacher used a similar opportunity to share her appreciation for the correction. She thanked the student for being willing to take a risk by speaking up and pointing out the error. Her appreciative reaction to one student let all her students know it is permissible to speak up and question the teacher in this classroom. She was also modeling the Responsible Action Statement, "Speak up for yourself."

"What a silly mistake that was."

A middle school science teacher, when informed of a mistake, confessed to the class, "What a silly mistake that was!" His intention was to show his humanness by making fun of himself.

Laughing at yourself can be used effectively on occasion. But making fun of yourself can easily backfire and be misinterpreted by students. By ridiculing himself, this teacher inadvertently informed the class that mistakes are silly and if you make them in this classroom ridicule could follow. Many youngsters could come away believing that people who make mistakes in this classroom will be made fun of.

"Let's stop a minute and see what we can learn from that error."

One high school teacher reacted to the public disclosure of his mistake by thanking the student for pointing it out and leading a discussion about what could be learned from that mistake. Conclusions in this secondary classroom included:

1. If you try to go too fast, errors happen.
2. Mistakes can be corrected.
3. Mistakes can lead to learning.
4. Mistakes are not good or bad. They are simply data that you can use to improve and grow.
5. Mistakes are valuable.
6. If you're not making some mistakes, maybe you're not learning anything.
7. You can't do anything about a mistake if you're not aware of it.
8. What you do after learning you made a mistake is your choice.
9. Erasers have a purpose, and they don't work by themselves.

Regardless of how you react to your own mistakes, students are learning important lessons from your behavior. What are your students learning from your reactions to your errors? Whatever reaction you choose in this important situation, you can be assured of one thing: your students are watching and learning something. Are you offering that lesson with intentionality? Are you purposefully defining that defining moment?

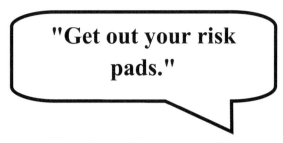

"On your risk pad, see if you can spell 'consensus.'"

"See if you can do this one in your head. Write the answer on your risk pad."

"Make a prediction and put it on your risk pad."

These are examples of Teacher Talk used by teachers who employ risk pads to make it safe for students to participate.

Some students choose to sit and do nothing rather than risk being wrong. They rarely volunteer an answer, look down when called on, and wait for the teacher to move on. They play it safe.

Spelling bees, board work, the red pencil, and publicly displayed achievement charts often have the effect of producing shame, embarrassment, ridicule, anxiety, and fear in students. As a result, some students withdraw, give up, and sit in your classroom doing nothing more than wearing paint off their chair.

Risk pads are one more way to bring the Responsible Action Statement, "Mistakes are permitted here," to life. This is a device to encourage and motivate students at any grade level to come out of their shell and participate. If it isn't safe to make a mistake on a risk pad, where is it safe?

> ## "Now stretch your answer even more."

Stretch and *challenge* are two additional words that signal to your students that this is a safe place.

"This one is the *challenge* problem. Are you willing to step up and take the *challenge?*"

"See if you can enjoy *stretching* your list of facts on this one."

When your Teacher Talk validates students who are willing to stretch themselves and accept challenges, you encourage more of that behavior. You increase the chances that they will be willing to step out of their previous routine of giving up and restricting their efforts in order to make changes necessary for growth and learning.

> ## "Let's see who can be first, best, fastest, do the most."

"Boys and girls, let's see who can make the best drawing."

"Michelle wins the star for our honor chart for the most work done correctly."

"The best essay on citizenship will be published in the school newspaper."

This kind of Teacher Talk reveals an inappropriate reliance on competition to motivate students.

Competition is EVERYWHERE in today's schools. We give awards for reading the most books, creating the best poster, and getting the most correct answers on a test. And we are overdoing it.

Competition can be useful and fun if students choose, rather than are required, to participate and if they are competing against students at the same skill level. Forced competition creates one winner and many losers. This might be fun for kids who have a chance to win and want to do some self-testing to see how they stack up. But for those who have no chance of winning it is counterproductive and elicits images of failure in their minds.

Competition does not lead to meaningful learning. Nor does it create lifelong learners. It helps children focus more on the extrinsic reward of winning and less on the desired learning.

Monitor your Teacher Talk for evidence of a reliance on competition. Use that information to help you keep competition in perspective. Reserve most of it for students who choose to compete in extracurricular activities.

We were recently told about a teacher who was informed of the negative effects of competition in the classroom. She set a professional development goal to change, but old habits don't die easily. When counseled to use more cooperative activities to replace the competitive ones she had been relying on, the teacher's response was to create a bulletin board that featured a public record-keeping system for who could be the *most* cooperative this week.

"It's time for partner work."

Wouldn't it be nice if it didn't matter at all to students who they had for a partner when cooperating on a shared assignment? Yes, it would be nice. What it really is, is a nice fantasy. It isn't going to happen. Students do care who they work with. Many want to work primarily with a few friends. Others prefer to work only with their best friend. Still others will work with anyone except Willy or Rolanda. Not enough students are gracious and mature enough to work happily with any of their classmates. That's why a structured process is necessary when you assign partners.

Part of your job in creating structure in your classroom is creating the form and ritual of assigning partners or groups. We have seen that done in several ways.

"Everybody find a partner."

"Everybody find a partner and come up with some ideas about why the main character in the story we read made that choice."

"Grab someone to be your partner and I'll tell you what to do next."

Delete such Teacher Talk from your instructional repertoire unless you want the same students to always be left out. No one picks them for a partner. Assigning partners is not a process that can be left to the students. This situation requires a more specific teacher structure.

Other methods we have observed teachers using to organize this important process include:

1. "The first row turn to the second row and the third row turn to the fourth row. The person across from you is your partner."

2. "Count off from one to twelve. When you get to twelve, start over. Now find someone in the room who has the same number as you do. He or she is your partner for this next activity."

3. "I will be passing out cards with a number on the back. Two of you will have the same number. Find that person and sit next to him or her for this activity."

4. "You will be getting a popsicle stick with a color on the end. Find the person who has the same color. That's your partner."

5. "Get out your Interaction Pal sheet. Today I want you to work with person number five on your list."

6. "On this chart I have assigned pairs. When I turn the cover sheet over you will find your name and the name of the person you will be working with today."

Any of the half-dozen ideas above is adequate for assigning partners. But none of them go far enough to insure mutual respect and emotional safety during the delicate partnering process. What is needed in each case is a "keep a straight face" lecture burst and direct teaching piece on the part of the teacher.

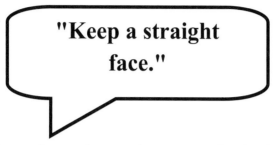

"I'm getting ready to assign partners for the day. As in the past, this is not your partner for the rest of the year or even for the entire month. This is the person to work with today when I ask you to share with a partner. You will only work with this person today. Tomorrow you'll have a different partner. In time, you will get an opportunity to work with all of your classmates.

"If you happen to be partnered with a friend today, you won't be tomorrow. If you don't get your best friend today, you will later. You will get to work with everyone in the class at one time or another.

"When you find out who your partner is, I don't want you to react verbally or nonverbally. No verbal reactions. When you find out who your partner is I don't want to hear any groans. Nor do I want to hear, 'Oh darn,' or 'That stinks.' Those verbal responses are not respectful of your classmates and do not create the accepting and affirming environment we're building in this classroom. I will not allow anyone in this classroom to say those things about you and I will not allow you to say them about anyone else.

Also refrain from saying, 'Yippee, I got a good one,' or 'Yes!' No positive comments. No negative comments.

"Nonverbally means no facial expressions or gestures. No eye rolling. No disgusted looks. No thumbs up. No smiles. I want you to keep a straight face. Let's practice that now. Everybody put on your straight face. Place your hand on your head. Now bring it down slowly across the front of your face, wiping off all expressions as you go. A couple of you are smiling. See if you can wipe that smile off your face.

"Looks like you all have it. Now let's practice the no verbal or nonverbal responses as I pull the map up and reveal today's partners."

By teaching students to keep a straight face in this situation, you teach them that disrespect will not be tolerated in your classroom. You help them appreciate that respect and tolerance are behaviors that all of us need to practice with intentionality and regularity in order to honor the diversity and uniqueness that exist in our classroom and in our world.

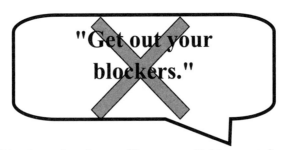

"It's time for the spelling test. Table captains, please get the blockers," requested the third-grade teacher. Six students immediately rose from their desks, walked to the cupboard, and took enough blockers to distribute to the students sitting at their table.

Constructed with three 8- by 10-inch sheets of cardboard taped together, blockers stand upright. They are designed to shield one student's paper from another's eyes.

This third-grade teacher thinks she is teaching spelling this morning. She is not. She is teaching students that they are cheaters. Her structure, using blockers, announces to every child in that classroom, "You can't be trusted. You are such cheaters that I have to design a structure that prevents it." Children learn the lessons communicated by your perceptions of them quickly and well.

> ## "It's time to activate our inside blockers."

Another third-grade teacher sees no need to use an external object to protect one child's paper from another's need to look. "It's time for our morning spelling test," she announces. "Remember, we are going to use our inside blockers again today. Looking or not looking at another's paper is an internal decision that each of you makes. It's something that happens on the inside of you. If each of you chooses to use your inside blocker, we don't need outside blockers. Choosing to practice honesty, integrity, respect, and caring is a decision that each of us makes on the inside. When you make an inside decision, the outside takes care of itself. Outside blockers are only needed when the inside blockers have not been turned on."

The spelling test proceeded and students practiced spelling words as they practiced using their inside blockers. Yes, they learned spelling. They also learned that they have the power to activate their inside blockers and that the teacher believes in their ability to do so.

Of the two teachers described above, which one do you think will attract the most cheating in her classroom?

It is our view that cheating (copying answers, using someone else's paper, etc.) is destructive and self-defeating behavior that has an adverse effect not only on the individual students but on the classroom as a whole. It is also our view that attempts to prevent cheating have undesirable effects. Here's why.

Teachers often use a variety of structured cheat-control techniques intended to head off cheating before it occurs. Such techniques include:

1. Arranging desks so students can't see another's paper.

2. Using blockers to prevent students from seeing what their classmates are writing.

3. Walking around the room during test periods saying things such as, "Keep your eyes on your own paper."

4. Having students exchange papers before correcting them.

Without question, teachers can reduce the amount of cheating that occurs in their classrooms by imposing such cheat-control techniques. Basically, more cheat control equals less cheating—an understandable equation that is used in classrooms throughout the world.

Firmly applied cheat-control measures can go a long way toward preventing the covert act from happening. Such measures may not eliminate cheating altogether, but they can certainly bring it under control. It will remain under control as long as the control remains.

But these measures are extrinsic; they come from a source outside the student. For that reason, they require rigorous and constant enforcement. Their effectiveness lasts only until the teacher's back is turned or he or she leaves the room for a moment.

"If I see you looking at another's paper, yours will go in the basket and you'll get a zero."

When we employ cheat-control strategies in our classrooms, we program students to look to us for control. We teach them that we, the authorities, are responsible for their behavior, and pass up precious opportunities to teach self-control and personal responsibility. We rob our students of the chance to develop their inner authority. In effect, we cheat our students by setting up situations in which they can't cheat.

Students are cheated because they miss a chance to grow in self-responsibility. They learn that others control their lives and are responsible for their actions. They become immersed in the protective shell of not having to take responsibility for themselves.

Our students would be better served if we eliminated the structure of cheat control as a preventive practice. It is precisely this type of prevention that prolongs the existence of cheating by forcing it underground.

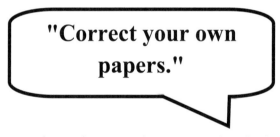

"Correct your own papers."

As an alternative to cheat control, give students opportunities to cheat. Let them correct their own papers. Use no blockers during spelling tests. Post answer keys on the wall. Design self-checking materials. Leave the teacher's edition on the resource table.

Begin by assuming no one will cheat. At the same time, know that some students probably will, since students have learned all too well the importance of right answers. Indeed, many have attached their feelings of self-worth to the number of correct answers they get on their papers.

When the barriers to cheating are dropped, remember that those who choose to cheat are not doing it because they are bad, or even dishonest. They're cheating because they haven't yet developed an inner authority that guides them to practice integrity. They have yet to discover the difference between the self-satisfaction of learning concepts and the insignificance of right answers. In short, they have more important lessons to learn than the spelling words or math problems that appear on their papers.

Once cheat control is ended, these students will demonstrate their need for personal growth. Identifying them will not be difficult. You will see him glancing at another student's paper or notice that she has the same exact answers as the person seated next to her. You will see a pattern of a student's having correct daily work and stumbling on retention checks. In essence, you will catch him or her cheating.

"Cathy, we need to have a talk about your math papers."

Once the "cheaters" are identified, you can begin to assist in their growth. Start by emotionally accepting them as they are, without judgment. Confer with these students privately. Refrain from showcasing your values by making "examples" of them. Share your concerns honestly, concentrating on your direct observations. Speak to the situation rather than to the character and personality of the student.

Work to fix the problem rather than to fix blame, and invite students into joint solution seeking. Keep the emphasis on the search for solutions rather than on blame and punishment. Help them to set goals and develop an action plan.

In addition to helping students choose honesty and integrity, you can work to control your own perceptions of cheating. When cheating occurs, it's possible to look at it from a variety of perspectives. You can view it as disgusting, dishonest, and immoral. If you do, you are likely to react by implementing regulations that prevent its recurrence. Or you can see cheating as a call for help and an opportunity for learning to take place. How you see it is up to you. What you do about it is also your choice.

"I'm going to use the name jar."

How do you decide who gets called on in your classroom? Do you call on only those who raise their hands? Do you keep track so everyone gets a fair chance to respond?

Consider using the name jar. The name jar contains slips of paper on which classroom members' names are written. When you ask a question, give the class a bit of thinking time. Then draw a name from the name jar and give the person whose name is picked a chance to respond.

Using the name jar in your classroom sends students important messages. They include:

1. I will not play favorites.
2. You will all have an equal opportunity to be called on.
3. Anyone could be called on at any moment.
4. You could be called on twice in a row, so be ready.
5. There is no need to raise your hand.
6. I want you to feel included and invited.

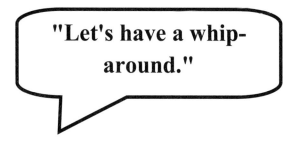

Another technique that works well to structure student responses and encourage involvement is the whip-around.

"Let's start at the end of this row and whip-around to Sarah in the back. Each person give a one-sentence reply telling what you think is the most important thing in this chapter. Remember that it's OK to pass."

Students go in turn up one row and down another, each giving his or her response. It is not necessary to whip-around the entire classroom. Just a portion will do. Alternate where you begin and end so everyone is included from time to time.

> ## "No hands in the air. Only writing."

"I'm going to pose a question," Joshua Kramer began. "I want you to write your answer on your risk pad. No hands in the air. If you are done writing before I call on anyone, see if you can expand on your answer. Who, in your opinion, was the most important character in the story and why do you think that? Please keep your answer to yourself. Silently record it on your risk pad. No hands in the air."

Joshua's Teacher Talk was so smooth that it would be easy to pass over the strength inherent in the structure. His verbal skill and intentionally chosen words created the following:

1. The need to be first with a hand in the air was eliminated, discouraging quick, surface-level responses.

2. Early finishers were encouraged to think more deeply.

3. All students were allowed thinking time.

4. Most students recorded an answer and had something to share if called on.

5. With a written answer in front of them, more students were likely to verbally share an answer.

6. If a student chose not to volunteer, at least he or she had an answer to compare with the others that were given.

Teachers who praise answers after students respond verbally have positive intentions. They think they are being supportive, encouraging, and helpful. They are not. Not if they're attempting to structure their classroom to create diversity in thinking.

Consider the following scenario.

Teacher: "What do you think Columbus would be doing if he were alive today?"

Student: "I think he would be an astronaut."

Teacher: "Good thinking, Arturo."

The "good thinking" comment coming from this teacher signals that Arturo has come up with the right answer. She has just increased the likelihood that the next few answers will be similar to Arturo's. At this point, many students stop thinking altogether. After all, Arturo has already done the "good thinking."

If encouraging diversity of thinking and creative responses is your goal, refrain from judging answers. Instead, use Teacher Talk that acknowledges and paraphrases.

Student: "I think he would be an astronaut."

Teacher: "So, something to do with the space industry."

This teacher's response acknowledges that she heard. She also paraphrased the student's answer to demonstrate her understanding of it. The answer was not judged, rated, or ranked. Now the class discussion can continue with students still thinking of responses, knowing theirs could be a right answer, too.

Student: "I think he would be an astronaut."

Teacher: "So, something to do with the space industry." (acknowledgement and paraphrase) "Who has another idea? Thomas."

Student: "I think he would be driving a truck."

Teacher: "A transportation focus then." (acknowledgement and paraphrase) "What's another one? Madison."

Student: "He could be a computer guy."

Teacher: "Exploring the Internet perhaps." (acknowledgement and paraphrase)

And so the conversation goes, with students coming up with diverse possibilities encouraged and supported by a teacher who skillfully structures her comments to affirm, acknowledge, and demonstrate that she heard.

Praise is appropriate if conformity is what you want. But if your goal is to encourage uniqueness and diversity, acknowledge and paraphrase.

> ## "What is ONE way their goods can be shipped to market?"

Does your Teacher Talk create a structure that encourages different right answers, or does it continually ask for the one correct answer?

Questions that require one right answer:
- Who was the fourth president of the United States?
- How do you spell refrigerator?
- How many oceans are there?

Questions that ask for different right answers:
- What is one way we could solve this problem?
- What possibilities exist for housing in this environment?
- What is one name we could give to our bunny?

When you ask a question that asks for different right answers, you ask students to think. They don't shut down their brains after one answer has been given. They're encouraged to explore and dig deeper. They come up with more unique and creative answers after the most obvious ones are exhausted.

Do your questions create a classroom structure that requires students to think or to recite?

"And what do you think about that, Miss Wilson?"

This question was asked by a teacher who noticed a student who was obviously not paying attention. This was the teacher's best effort to communicate the importance of paying attention and get the student back on task. His best effort was not good enough.

This type of Teacher Talk takes everyone's attention off the task at hand and gives it to the person not paying attention. Now *all* students are focused off task. In addition, this attempt to publicly embarrass a student often elicits a defensive or silly reaction. Continued silence or resentment are other possible outcomes of this verbal challenge.

As an alternative, use proximity behavior. Walk toward the student and stand close to her as you continue to teach. If her behavior does not change, tell her quietly and privately what you expect. Or say respectfully, "Brenda, please make a different choice."

> ## "That would be an interesting topic for another day."

Did you ever notice how some students are masters at changing the subject? They can do this especially well when you're confronting them about a behavior or bringing up some unpleasant issue.

"Remember when we had the guest speaker last month?" a student might ask, attempting to get you to reminisce about a previously enjoyed moment. "I like that you help us learn the important parts of history," another might try in an effort to tell you something that you would like to hear.

Be on guard for the student who changes the subject to divert attention from your main mission. Simply go back to the beginning and use effective Teacher Talk to restate your intention. "Richard, that could be an interesting topic for another day, and right now I want to talk about your effort in geometry."

Be polite, firm, and serious without adding anger or frustration. "Sabrina, sounds like you want to talk about volleyball. I want to talk about blurting out in class. Let's get back to the main agenda. When you blurt out in class without raising your hand I get frustrated because other students don't get the time they need to think about an answer, and they don't get an equal opportunity to respond."

Firmly bring the conversation back to your main agenda as many times as you need to. Eventually, the student will see that you're sticking to the structure and will deal with your priority item.

> **"Let's give Ahmed the silent cheer."**

A silent cheer is having students energetically wave their arms around and scream silently. This is done to celebrate a student's effort, accomplishment, or completion of a task. This ritual requires little time, can be spontaneous, and helps build the supportive atmosphere that you're attempting to structure. Plus, it's fun!

Other celebrations we learned from the Performance Learning Systems graduate course, Classroom Management: Orchestrating a Community of Learners, include:

- Have each student touch an index finger to another person's index finger while saying, "YYYeeessss!"
- Have students move their arms around in a circular motion while clapping their hands, thus giving a "round" of applause.

> **"Let's revisit something we learned earlier this semester."**

It was a crowded restaurant, so full that I (Chick) had to give my name to the hostess and wait in the lobby until my name was called. Several others who had preceded me in line had not yet been seated, so I had to stand. It was there, standing in the waiting area minding my own business, that I noticed her.

She must have been around five or six years old. She was sitting next to her mother, waiting to be called for dinner. She had already received three crayons and a paper to work on, the kind of paper that restaurants give kids to keep them busy until their meal arrives. It contained riddles, an escape-from-the-dungeon challenge, a word search, and a dot-to-dot adventure.

I watched as she worked on the dot-to-dot picture. The numbers went from one to fifty. It was obvious to me that the dots, when connected, would make an elephant. When the youngster got to number ten, which clearly showed the head of an elephant, I asked her, "Do you know what that's going to be?"

"Yep," she replied.

"What?" I questioned.

"An elephant."

"Looks like one to me, too," I offered.

Torn between minding my own business and proceeding with the conversation, I chose to ask one more question.

"Well, if you already know it's going to be an elephant, why are you still connecting those dots instead of doing some of the other activities on your paper?"

She looked at me as though I were from another planet and replied, "'Cause I'm good at it." End of discussion.

Later, I thought about that incident and the little girl who did things because she was good at them. I thought about school and how we usually have kids work on the things they are not good at. In fact, in most schools, one of the rewards for getting good at something is that a student no longer gets to work on it.

If a child working on multiplication tables masters the threes and fours, she is given fives and sixes. If she then masters the fives and sixes, she is immediately moved on to sevens and eights. Some reward!

If a student learns addition, he goes on to subtraction. When he learns that, it's on to multiplication. The reward for learning something a student doesn't know is, "Here's something else you don't know. Work on that for a while."

Of course we need to help students learn things they don't know. And most class time should probably be spent on that. But couldn't we create a classroom structure that includes some time in which students can work on things they already know?

Wouldn't there be some value in having students who are working on their eights and nines go back and do their twos and threes? It would give them a sense of how far they've come—a yardstick with which to measure their own progress as learners. It might help them realize, "These are easy. I remember when they were hard. Maybe the hard eights and nines will seem easy someday."

We like to do what we're good at, too. Don't you? We love leading seminars, writing books, and working with children because we're good at those things. We bet the same concept holds true for you.

Why not provide some time each week or each semester for students to revisit what they previously learned? Let them go back and play around with what was taught the first two weeks of the semester. Devote some time on Monday to letting them burn through some easy material that once was hard. Debrief with them afterward, checking out what they thought about it. You just might find they enjoyed themselves because they were good at it.

THE VOICE OF NURTURE

The voice of nurture is needed to demonstrate concern, caring, and genuine interest in students' well-being. This involves building relationship through the use of empathy, understanding, and mutual respect.

"My job is to teach, not build relationship," a frustrated teacher informed us at one of our frequent educator seminars. A meaningful response to that was not difficult to articulate. We used our own recommendations and gave her nurture first, followed by information.

"It would be nice if we could just concentrate on the teaching voice," Thomas began, leading with empathy. "It's tough to nurture when you'd rather be teaching." Having modeled the voice of nurture, he then gave the teacher this important teaching piece that explains why learning to skillfully use that voice is important.

A student's motivation to behave comes from being in a relationship. The number one reason why kids behave in school and work to achieve is because they are in relationship with an adult they look up to and respect and don't want to disappoint. You can lengthen the school year, test every other week, narrow the curriculum, implement test-prep strategies, raise the standards, or use any other strategy you can think of to restructure schools. The fact remains, what matters most is the relationship between one student and one teacher.

The nurturing voice is soft and gentle. It shows concern for the student. This important voice recognizes and responds to feelings as well as to words. It strives to create connection even if the student is in full tantrum mode. It embodies empathy, listening, presence, eye contact, appropriate touch, pleasant tone, and skillful verbal responses.

The verbal skills and teacher behaviors detailed in this chapter will help you put the voice of nurture to use in your professional practice.

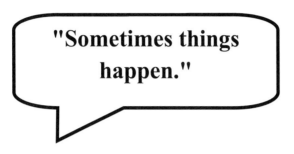

"Sometimes things happen."

Kindergarten. First day of school. Excitement. Too much excitement, perhaps. A five-year-old pooped his pants. The teacher knew. Kindergarten teachers know these things.

No, it wasn't raw intuition that tipped her off. Neither was it the fact that the child dropped his head into the shame position when he stood before her. It was one of her other senses that supplied the main clue. She could smell it.

"Sometimes things happen," she said, as she began to deal with this awkward first-day-of-school moment. Not her first day, but his. It was his first day ever at this school, with this teacher, with these students.

Do you smell something besides poopy pants? Do you smell the potential for this kid getting off to a really bad start on a very important day in his life? This teacher did.

"Let's talk, just you and me, over here," she suggested. "Everybody has accidents," she continued when they were alone. "I'll take care of you. It's going to be OK. I have clean clothes for you that will fit you just right. When you're done changing your clothes, come join us in the classroom." She saw the relieved look on his face. And he saw the accepting look on hers. Here was a teacher who knew that nurture often includes both words and actions.

"Let me know if you need any other help," she said quietly. He nodded his head and entered the bathroom. He didn't need any other help. His day had been saved. He returned to the classroom a few minutes later with new clothes and his dignity intact.

> **"What an honor that he chose to land on you."**

Some kids are afraid of bugs. Others are not. Some teachers are afraid of bugs. Others are not. So it was not an insignificant situation when a bug recently landed on the shoulder of an unsuspecting second-grader.

The bug wasn't noticed by the child the bug had selected as a landing pad. Other children noticed and began acting agitated. When the teacher realized what was happening, she immediately stopped the class and used her voice of nurture.

"Oh, my goodness! Look at this. You are *so fortunate!* What an *honor* that he chose to land on you. Let me just help you," she said as she swept up the offending vermin with her bare hand. She then showed it to the children and pointed out its bug anatomy. Later, she walked to the door and gently released the insect outside.

How did the children react as this teacher responded to the bug? They stopped in their tracks and their agitation ceased as fear was replaced with fascination. The targeted child never spooked. Embarrassment was averted. Instead, he appeared to be happy to be in the spotlight. Nurture can create that.

Before the bug was released, this teacher helped her students learn two important lessons. First, the careful examination of the insect taught them about the importance of scientific observation. Second, they learned that unexpected circumstances do not have to be the signal for hysterical behavior.

This teacher transformed what could have been an embarrassing, fearful incident into an opportunity for learning and for an honor to be bestowed on a student chosen by a bug. She is clearly a skilled nurturer.

> **"I can see you boys are angry."**

Two kindergarten students came bursting out of the school bus pushing, shoving, and loudly proclaiming their existence. As they entered the schoolroom door they continued their struggle. In an instant they were sprawled on the floor kicking, slugging, grabbing, and hollering.

The teacher went immediately to the two boys and separated them with gentle firmness. "I can see you boys are angry," she stated.

"I can see you boys are angry" were her exact words. No more. No less. But the message she communicated far exceeded the brevity of her comment. Although the words she spoke were, "I can see you boys are angry," the real message was, "I recognize your feelings. It looks to me like anger. I am not afraid of your anger. I see it and I respect it. Your anger is an honest emotion and you are entitled to it. I won't try to deny your anger or change it. It is OK to be angry here."

> **"Show me just how angry you are."**

After the teacher stated, "I can see you boys are angry," the boys nodded ("Yes, we are angry"). The teacher then took both boys by the hand and led them to a woodworking center. She pulled out a box of scrap lumber, some nails, and two hammers. "Now show me just how angry you are," she challenged.

The boys responded. Angry noise filled the room as hammers alternately hit and missed nails. A few moments later the nail hammering ended. The boys tired of the task and found other activities to experience.

What is important here is that this skilled professional educator used the voice of nurture to show two boys an appropriate way to express their anger. She showed them that anger in itself is not bad, but some ways of expressing it could not be tolerated in this setting. She provided them with a legitimate channel through which to communicate their feelings.

Most discipline challenges consist of two parts: angry feelings and angry acts. Each part has to be handled differently. A simple rule of thumb here is, set limits on acts and do not restrict feelings.

> ## "You seem extremely frustrated."

Children today, tots to teens, are starving for feeling recognition. Their feelings need to be identified and expressed.

"You look sad."

"You are anxious."

"That looks like annoyance to me."

While feelings do need to be identified and expressed, certain behaviors may well need to be limited and/or redirected.

> ## "You can feel angry, and you don't get to call him names."

"You can be as angry as you choose with Mrs. Wilhelm, and you'll get yourself in a lot of trouble if you run a key across her car."

"Cassandra is not for punching. Show me with this doll how you're feeling."

"Pencils are not for throwing. Stomp your feet and tell me how angry you are."

The voice of nurture responds to a student on the feeling level. It acknowledges and paraphrases feelings. When coupled with the teaching of the appropriate behavior, the results are often dramatic and immediate.

When a student is caught up in the midst of strong emotion, it is not the time to give advice, soothe feelings, give constructive feedback, console, or engage in solution seeking.

THEY CANNOT HEAR YOU!

Let us make this really clear. *When a student is caught up in the midst of strong emotion, THEY CANNOT HEAR YOU!*

A student in tantrum mode is in the animal part of his or her brain. The frontal lobe of the brain is where listening, rational thought, and solution seeking occur. A student in the animal part of his brain is caught in an emotional meltdown that shuts off thinking.

Sorry, but your words will fall on deaf ears.

Teaching, preaching, reassuring, and problem solving will not work when a student is drowning in emotionality. The timing is off. When a person in water is going under and flailing around helplessly, it is not the time to give him swimming lessons.

To get the student back to his frontal lobe, be quiet and listen. Attend with your body. Nurture with your presence. Give him strong eye contact and present an open body posture. Get down on his level physically and do not interrupt the narrative. When the student stops talking, paraphrase what you heard and saw.

Say, "You feel _____ because _____."

Or ask, "Are you feeling _____ because _____?"

At this point the student will often answer, "That's right," or tell you, "No, I'm not mad. I'm furious!" Paraphrase again, saying, "So it's stronger than mad. You're furious because _____." Now you are in a dialog, which signals the move back toward the frontal lobe. By nurturing through listening, presence, and effective verbal skills, you have set the stage to move to solution seeking, making amends, or returning to the task at hand.

But what if they don't tell me how they're feeling, you might wonder.

"You seem sad."

With young children especially, you might need to help them find the appropriate feeling word. Mad, sad, glad, and scared are the four basic feelings. Start there.

Say, "You seem scared." "You look glad." "You seem really mad." If you aren't accurate, children will often tell you.

Later, you can introduce bigger feeling words into their vocabulary.

"You look agitated."

"You seem annoyed."

"You might be flabbergasted."

This is the beginning of emotional intelligence. Important ingredients of emotional intelligence are knowing the names of your feelings, how to recognize them, and how to handle them constructively.

Sadly, we don't teach emotional intelligence in many schools today. You know why. It isn't on the test.

> ## "Help me understand what you're feeling."

If you aren't sure how a student is feeling, ask. To do this effectively, you must change your goal from one of fixing the situation to one of understanding how the student is feeling. Understanding needs to precede fixing in order to maintain and strengthen the relationship between you and the student. Fixing can come later, after understanding has been achieved. Nurture. Then fix.

> **"Your teeth are clenched and your hands are so tight your knuckles are turning white."**

If the student does not or cannot articulate a feeling, paraphrase what you see and hear. With a teenager, it might sound like this:

"You're so upset you can't stop yelling. You look like you want to hit someone. There is fire in your eyes and your jaw is tight. Your voice is getting louder and louder."

With a younger child, it might sound like this:

"I see your arms and legs kicking and waving. You're breathing hard and having trouble talking. You seem angry. Your hands are gripping your blouse and I see your tears."

Continue to use Teacher Talk that paints a picture of her behavior. Be descriptive. Adding judgments and inferences will only intensify the tantrum. Somewhere in the process of your describing her behavior, the student will give you eye contact. This is a signal that she's beginning to reaccess her frontal lobe. Use this opportunity to suggest a feeling. "You seem really sad."

If she launches back into tantrum mode, return to paraphrasing what you see and hear. Wait for eye contact and repeat the process. Repeat as often as necessary until you've engaged a conversation. Once you have nurtured this student back into her frontal lobe you can move to the voice of teaching, debriefing, or accountability as we discuss later in the book.

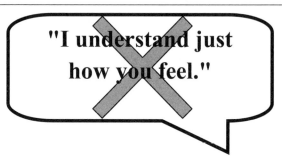

When your student is caught up in strong emotion, it is not time to *tell* her you understand; it is time to *demonstrate* that you understand.

To demonstrate that you understand, you must first listen. Then paraphrase what you heard or saw. You need to prove that you understand by listening carefully and reflecting back what you think you heard. If you cannot do that, you did not listen well enough. When you get confirmation that you heard correctly, the student knows that you understand.

Don't just tell her you understand. Prove it.

> **"Alec, you seem upset."**

There are times when a student is not in tantrum mode but is sending nonverbal signals indicating some degree of distress. You may see a clenched fist or a defiant stare. These and other clues signal an angry, frustrated student. At times, it's helpful to give students who seethe with anger an opportunity to vent.

When you can, talk to the student privately. Use Teacher Talk that communicates that you recognize and honor the student's feelings. With a gentle yet concerned tone, say, "Alec, you seem upset. I may or may not be picking up your feelings accurately, but I'm wondering if you'd like to talk about it."

Giving a person who is full of emotion an opportunity to share those feelings serves as a relief valve to release pressure before it explodes. Don't allow strong student emotion to boil over. Use your Teacher Talk skills to avoid an explosion by saying, "Brenda, I'm picking up some angry vibes from you. Help me understand what you're feeling."

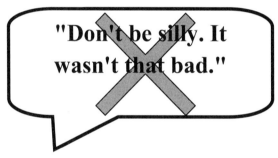

"Don't be silly. It wasn't that bad."

Showing empathy for your students' feelings is one of the most important verbal skills you can learn as an educator. It will invite them to feel respected, seen, heard, honored and understood.

Too often, teachers attempt to change their students by talking them out of their feelings.

"You shouldn't be scared."

"Boys don't cry."

"Come on. Get over it."

"You're overreacting."

"You're too sensitive. Don't let it bother you."

These sorts of phrases do not nurture. Instead, they create a disconnect between the teacher and student. The student often feels misunderstood and invalidated and perceives a lack of support from an important adult in her life.

If you hear what the student is feeling, honor it, reflect it (paraphrase), and do not try to change it, the strong emotion often subsides. Nurture can do that.

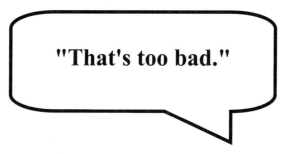

"That's too bad."

When a student comes to you with a problem, nurture by leading with empathy.

"Bummer."

"What a shame."

"I'm sorry that happened to you."

"Yes, that can be hard sometimes."

Jean Paul confessed to his teacher that he hadn't had time to finish his assignment the previous night. Arturo told the band director that he forgot his white shirt for the concert. Mary Lou told her teacher she forgot her lunch and asked to call home.

Jean Paul's teacher reminded him that he had been given two days to complete the assignment. The band director told Arturo, "You know the rules. No shirt, no participation in the concert." Mary Lou's teacher informed her that this was the third time this had happened since the school year began. All three teachers missed an important opportunity to lead with empathy.

When a student brings you a problem, concern, or difficult situation, stop. Measure your words. Resist the urge to lead with reminders, mental scorekeeping, and/or teaching. Instead, go immediately to empathy to show concern for the student.

"That's too bad. You've got a tough one there. Sorry about that." An empathetic response builds connectedness. It communicates that relationship comes first. It announces, "Your feelings are important to me. The problem is secondary. Let me honor your feelings and then we can examine the situation." Concern for the person needs to precede concern for the problem. Information, teaching, or holding students accountable can follow empathy and will be more readily received once the student knows you care.

One of your students is moving. This is her last day in your classroom. She begins to cry softly at her desk. At this point, you have a variety of possible verbal responses available.

You could say, "It'll be okay, honey. Lots of kids move," or "Don't worry. Lots of good things will happen at the new school." This language, although well-intentioned, does not acknowledge feelings or help the child feel heard and understood. It does not nurture.

You may move closer to her, extend warm eye contact, pat her on the back and state lovingly, "I know it doesn't seem like it now, but you will make lots of new friends." Nice try, but still not helpful. You may have empathy in your tone. It may even show on your face. Still, your words are void of nurture.

"I bet it feels sad to leave here, and a bit scary" is a verbal expression of empathy. Coupled with a warm tone and gentle touch, this statement might help the student relax into the moment. It might also induce more tears. If the tears come, know they flow because you helped the child feel safe enough to express her feelings without having someone attempt to talk her out of them. Congratulations.

> **"Equations can be very frustrating, can't they?"**

You just explained an important concept about equations to Robert for the sixth time. His minimal efforts have not produced positive results. He looks up at you and whines, "I can't do it. It's too hard." What are you going to say in response? How are you going to react?

"Sure you can. I believe in you. Come on, try," at first glance looks like an encouraging response. It is not. This piece of Teacher Talk leapfrogs over empathy and goes directly to attempting to talk a student into believing in himself. You missed the most important step. You skipped the emotionality being expressed by the student and went straight to communicating on a cognitive level. You failed to nurture.

Do you think, "This was hard for me, too, when I was your age," is reassuring? Nope. It is another thinly veiled attempt to talk a student out of his feelings by using yourself as an example. Also, the conversation and attention has now moved to you and away from this student and his feelings.

"Equations can be very frustrating, can't they?" is Teacher Talk that leads with empathy. It honors the child's feelings first and keeps the focus of attention on the student and what he is experiencing emotionally.

"You should know by now that I'm not the same as every other teacher."

As you're in the process of reminding students of your expectation in regard to an important procedural issue, a tenth-grader in the back of the room blurts out, "Other teachers don't make us do that."

"You should know by now that I'm not the same as every other teacher" may seem to you like a simple reminder of the differences among teachers. Perhaps it is. And it is definitely *not* an example of effective nurturing. Your reminder ignores the feeling behind the student's statement and focuses on an explanation. Explanations can come later, after you demonstrate that you heard on a feeling level.

"Sounds like you think this is unfair" speaks to the feeling underneath the student's statement. By leading with an empathetic response you help the child feel understood and simultaneously lay the groundwork for her being willing to listen to your explanatory information.

> **"I'm sad that happened. If anyone can handle it, you can."**

Wilson Alverez, a tenth-grader, forgot to wear his white shirt and black pants on the day of the choir concert. In the past, students without proper dress had not been able to participate. Wilson went immediately to the choir director and explained his problem. That's when Wilson heard these words from his teacher: "I'm sad that happened. If anyone can handle it, you can."

The words that came out of the teacher's mouth in this situation were, "I'm sad that happened. If anyone can handle it, you can." Yet the real messages, the silent messages beneath those spoken words, went far beyond what was actually voiced by the teacher. The implied messages included:

"I feel empathy for you."
"This is your problem."
"I believe in your ability to handle it."
"Whatever you decide, I know you can cope."
"I see you as a solution seeker."
"I know you can think for yourself."

"I will not rescue you, save you, bail you out, or give you one more last chance."

"I care enough to hold you accountable, so I will allow you to experience the outcome your actions created."

"Learning how to deal with mistakes is as important as learning the lyrics."

"Oh, my. I see tears."

When one student manifests aggression toward another, it's time to move in. The aggression could take the form of a first-grader pushing another child off the swing. It could be a fourth-grader hitting a classmate with her fist. Or the aggression could manifest as one middle school student tripping another intentionally. Regardless of the form the aggression takes, the role of the teacher is to move in immediately.

Most of the time, educators go immediately to the aggressor. We chase after the perpetrator. Regardless of what we tell him or her, at this point we're talking to the wrong person. When there is an act of aggression, go to the receiver (victim) first.

Going to the aggressor first teaches him or her that aggression is a guaranteed way to get attention in your classroom. This shows both the receiver and the aggressor that you value aggression more than injury. It reveals that your first priority is to focus on attacking rather than on healing.

That message will not be missed by anyone involved. Your students will notice. They will get the message.

Go to the receiver (victim) first and communicate empathy for what has happened to him. Use language that shows the receiver that you see the world through his eyes.

- Begin by reflecting a feeling. "You seem sad."
- Describe what happened. "You were swinging away and all of a sudden got an unexpected push in the back. You landed hard in the dirt."
- Add more empathy. "I'm sorry that happened to you."
- Describe the effect. "I see tears on your face and scratches on your hands."
- Reflect a feeling. "That must be frustrating."

Once you have communicated with the receiver and handled the injury, you can go to the aggressor. Now you have an opportunity to use the voice of teaching (described fully in chapter three). "Jason, that was pushing. We don't do that here because it isn't safe and people like Jermaine can get hurt. When we want a turn on the swing in this school, we go up to the other person and tell them, 'I'd like a turn on the swing. Will you please tell me when you're done.'"

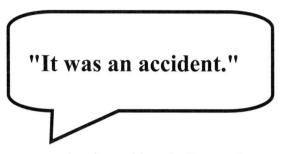

"It was an accident."

Some aggression is accidental. One student accidentally steps on another's foot as he goes to sharpen his pencil. Another trips and bumps a classmate in the drinking fountain line. Your job here is to use language that shows empathy and lets both students know this was an accident.

"You seem angry. Yoshi was walking down the aisle and stepped right on your foot. That can hurt. It was an accident."

"I see your anger. Carin was standing behind you in the line and Jessica bumped her and she bumped you. I'm glad no one was hurt. It was an accident."

The words "It was an accident" are crucial to help students become conscious of the difference between accidental and intentional aggression. Add them to your growing repertoire of effective Teacher Talk.

> ## "Good morning, Esther."

Greeting time is an important opportunity to nurture. Do you invest the time to greet each student as he or she arrives? Do you call your students by name as they enter your room? Do you stand by the door and deliver a warm smile?

Jason Weirans taught fourth grade. He greeted students every day. He called many of them by name. He just forgot one thing. He forgot to look at them.

Jason was busy putting work on the board as children arrived. He glanced up, saw who entered, and gave a friendly greeting. Yet he spoke with his back to the students. Occasionally a student would come to him and ask a question as he wrote the morning assignments. Being what he considered a great multitasker, Jason answered the question as he continued to finish his work at the board. In the process, he missed an important facet of nurturing: use of his eyes and facial expressions.

Yes, using nurturing words is important. So is the tone and volume of your voice. And equally important is attending with your body, which includes facing the student and extending eye contact coupled with a warm expression.

Be present when you nurture or you will lose many of the benefits that can accrue when you give attention to building positive relationships.

> ## "I noticed you were at the basketball game last night."

Recently, the staff at a West Coast middle school (grades 7-9) set a school goal of improving relationships between teachers and students. The teachers in the school hold high expectations for their students academically. They expect them to achieve, and they know that demanding rigor from students without having them feel connected to teachers is folly. So they set out to improve the relationship portion of the relationship/rigor connection. They labeled their efforts the Silent Mentor Program.

At the beginning of the year, all the eighth-graders were surveyed in an effort to find out how many students felt they'd had a positive relationship with a teacher during the previous year and how many felt they had not. The students were given a list of teachers' names and were asked to circle the ones they felt they had a positive relationship with. Having a positive relationship was defined as being able to talk to the teacher and feeling comfortable asking for his or her help. It also included a feeling that the teacher liked them based on the interest the teacher showed in the student.

One hundred and twenty-one eighth-grade students filled out the forms. Some students listed several teachers. Others mentioned one or two. Twenty-five middle-schoolers listed no teacher they felt they had a positive relationship with.

The information gleaned from the survey was tabulated and shared with the teachers. The teachers were provided with two sheets of information. One had a list of the twenty-five students who listed no teacher. The other sheet, given privately to each educator, had the teacher's name at the top and listed the students who identified them as someone they felt they had a positive relationship with.

Some teachers received a page which showed that no student had selected them. The School Improvement Committee thought every teacher needed to know how they were perceived by the students. So they simply gave the teachers that information privately.

At this point, each professional staff member was asked to select one student from the list who had indicated no relationship with a teacher the previous year. The student they chose would become their silent mentee. It was called "silent" because no one told the mentees they had been chosen. Each mentor (teacher) had one mentee (student). Care was taken to make sure that each student was selected by someone and that each teacher had a different student.

Throughout the year, teachers were asked to reach out in special ways to nurture their mentee. Each Monday the School Improvement Committee gave the teachers a new task to complete during the week. The first week they were asked to send their silent mentee three "I noticed" statements, such as:

"I noticed you like to wear red."

"I noticed you came to school in a new car today."

"I noticed you had a big smile on your face this morning."

The words out of the mentors' mouths were, "I noticed," but the real message in such statements is, "I see you. You are not going to be invisible here."

Notice that the statements above are positive and void of evaluation, unlike, "I noticed you did a good job on that," or "I noticed your paper was sloppy."

This nurturing verbal skill is not about evaluation. It is about communicating, "I see you."

> **"Thank you for sharing that, Charles."**

The following week, the mentors were asked to use the mentee's name at least once a day for the entire week. We have heard it said that the sweetest sound in any language is the sound of our own name. We agree. You can indeed build intimacy and relationship with the nurturing technique of using students' names.

Use names at the beginning of a sentence. "Ahmed, do you have a reaction to that?" Use names in the middle of a sentence. "That fact you put in there, Marie, helped me understand the point you were making." Use names at the end of a sentence. "That was right on target, Emilio."

> **"Kelly, give me a high-five."**

On another Monday, the Committee asked mentors to give their mentees two physical touches during the week. These could include a high-five, a pat on the back, a shoulder squeeze, a fist bump or a handshake. Notice that these recommended touches are all quick and require a minimum of physical contact. Appropriate physical touch is a positive way to nurture that demonstrates caring, affection, concern, and interest.

One second-grade teacher we know gives students a choice at the end of each day. "As you leave," she tells them, "you can give me a thumbs-up, a high-five, or a hug." In this way she gives students control over the degree of touch they receive while insuring that she connects physically with every student every day.

"Estaban, will you help me with this?"

Another strategy employed by the silent mentors one week, as assigned by the Committee, was asking the student for help at least twice during the week.

Asking someone for help tells them you value their expertise, trust their ability, or appreciate their strengths. It says, "I believe I can count on you."

> **"I'm thinking about getting a dog. Do you think a cocker spaniel would be good in an apartment?"**

Another week, the teachers in the Silent Mentor Program were asked to seek their mentee's opinion about a topic, situation, or problem. Issuing a minimum of three opinion-seeking invitations was suggested.

You can ask a student about your favorite football tcam, a television program, a hairstyle, a movie, or a topic of your choice. You don't have to follow her advice or use his idea or suggestion. You just have to elicit it. People feel a closer connection to people who seek their opinion.

After you ask, listen. Be interested enough to listen to the student when she responds to you.

> **"Circle the names of the teachers you felt you had a meaningful relationship with this year."**

Other strategies used by the silent mentors that year were:

1. **Give the student the OK sign or a wink a specified number of times**. (Notice that this idea and the ones listed previously are not extravagant suggestions. They cost no money. You don't have to wait for them to come in the mail. And they don't take exorbitant amounts of time to implement.)

2. **Send one eye hug per day this week**. An eye hug is sustained eye contact ending with a smile. Begin by touching the student with your eyes. Giving extended eye contact says, "I care about you. You're important to me." Little or no eye contact communicates, "I don't care. Right now something else is more important to me." End with a smile. After you have held the student's gaze for a few seconds, give a broad smile.

Many children today have iPhones, iPods and the like. What many of them really need is an iHug.

One caution here. While you work at giving extended, direct eye contact to students, do not insist they make eye contact with you. There are cultures represented in classrooms today where eye contact with an adult is considered a sign of disrespect. Looking away from a person in authority or looking down is a way some children have been taught to respect elders.

In addition, eye contact heightens intimacy. Allow the student to determine the degree of intimacy and risk that he or she is willing to engage. Give eye contact, invite eye contact, and DO NOT require eye contact.

3. Be in the student's proximity three times during the week (other than in the classroom) was another assignment mentors found in their school mailbox one Monday. "Strategic placement," as it's sometimes called, means being in the vicinity of the student you wish to influence. Simply be in his or her vicinity more often that you normally would. You don't have to DO anything. You just have to BE there.

All of the techniques used in the Silent Mentor Program were recycled throughout the year. At the end of the year, students completed the initial survey again. "Circle the names of the teachers you felt you had a meaningful relationship with this year," they were instructed by the School Improvement Committee.

At the end of their seventh-grade year, EVERY STUDENT indicated that he or she was in a positive relationship with at least one teacher. This included the twenty-five who had previously mentioned no one. Many them listed more than one teacher this time. In addition, EVERY TEACHER was named by two or more students.

Do you want a working definition of "No child left behind"? This is it. With the Silent Mentor Program, this staff left NO child behind. And by leaving no child behind, they took every teacher right along with them.

Every student and every teacher was on someone else's list. Congratulations to that school staff!

Thanks to the professional educators on this staff and their understanding of the important connection between rigor and relationship, rigor now has a better chance of having an impact on their middle school students. Take a bow, you guys.

> **"I am Mr. Wilson and I teach government. I think I know most of you, and I'm happy to have you here in class."**

These are the first words spoken to students every year by Gerard Wilson, a twelve-year teaching veteran. He isn't kidding when he says, "I think I know most of you."

We were attracted to his story and his circumstances during a lunch conversation we had in one of our workshops when he stated matter-of-factly, "I don't have any trouble with troublemakers. They behave pretty well in my classroom."

It wasn't just *our* ears that perked up when Gerard made that statement about troublemakers. The other teachers at the table reacted as well. Everyone leaned in a bit and encouraged him to go on. Over the next half hour the following story emerged as a result of our questions and his forthright answers.

"I get every student who comes through our high school," he began. "They all have to take government. It's a requirement for graduation. My plan is simple. I find out who the troublemakers are early in their high school careers and build relationship with them for three years before they even get me as a teacher. By the time they come into my class they already know I'm a good guy."

With some prodding, Gerard explained how he identified the troublemakers. His identification system is simple. "I listen in the staff room when other teachers begin complaining," he said. "They talk about these students all the time. It's not difficult to determine who the teachers are having trouble with. I make a list of ten to twelve students in each grade level that the teachers are complaining about. Then I build relationship with them for several years."

So how does Gerard Wilson build relationship with students who are causing trouble in other teachers' classrooms? With the following activities, which he calls his Super Seven Relationship Builders. Notice the similarities between these high school strategies and the ones described previously in the Silent Mentor Program in a middle school.

1. "I give them two 'I noticed . . .' statements per week. I want them to know I know who they are. I want them to know that I'm friendly."
2. "I give them one physical touch per week. My desire is to show concern and caring through physical touch. I give them a high-five, a pat on the back, a light shoulder squeeze, or a handshake."
3. "I get close to them once a week. I sit near them at an assembly, stand behind them in the lunch line, or walk near them as they pass in the hallway. Often I don't even say anything. I'm just there in their line of sight."
4. "I smile at them twice a week."
5. "I give them a thumbs-up, the OK sign, or a hand wave once a week."

6. "I touch them with my eyes. I try to hold their gaze for a few seconds."

7. "I use their names. 'Hello, Mary.' 'Juan, looks like you got a haircut.' I want them to know that I'm aware of them even as freshmen."

"I keep a file card on each of the students I've identified," Gerard told the teachers at the lunch table. "I make sure I do three of the things on my Super Seven Relationship Builders list each week with each student. If I don't have three check marks on a card by Friday, I go looking for that student."

By the time a student takes government, Gerard has had three years worth of relationship-building contacts with him or her. The student is familiar with him as a person and has developed a positive connection. So if he chooses to enforce the school rules or hold students accountable for the choices they made, he does so in the context of a positive relationship that has already been well established.

The other teachers in his building often experience problems with many of the students that create no problems for Gerard Wilson. That phenomenon is no accident. It happens because this teacher set out with intentionality to create it with three years of positive nurturing.

"I'm enjoying the seriousness with which many of you are taking this."

"That was fun for me. I hope it was fun for you, too."

"I met many of your parents last night for the first time. They are deeply interested in you and your school work."

"I noticed how clean you left the lunchroom today. That makes cleanup a lot easier."

Teachers and administrators in one Pennsylvania school are increasing the number of positive responses they give to students and to one another. This staff has instituted TONE Week. TONE, an acronym for "Turn On Nice Expressions," is an effort by the entire staff to speak in ways that communicate respect for students and increase the number of positive comments to which they are exposed. Naturally, the positive comments are nurturing and delivered with a positive tone.

> **"All of you would like my attention right now."**

"Wow! So many of you would like to be first."

"I hear you would like me to put off the test until next week."

How do you nurture when students ask the impossible? What kind of nurture would be helpful when a student wants something you are not going to grant? What do you say now?

Grant their wish in fantasy. Let them know it is not possible in reality.

Seven students crowded the second-grade teacher's desk wanting to show her their picture. There is no way this teacher can look at all the pictures at the same time. It is not possible in reality. Yet it is possible in fantasy.

"Wow! So many of you want to be first," she began. "All of you would like my attention right now. I would like that, too. I wish you could all be first." This grants their wish in fantasy. Since it couldn't be granted in reality, she continued, "That would be nice, but I can only look at one at a time. I'm going to start here beside me with Tommy and go right around my desk so everyone can have a turn. I want to see all of your pictures."

When middle school students begged to have the test put off until Monday, their teacher granted them their wish in fantasy. "I hear you would like me to put off the test until next week. Wouldn't that be a relief? In fact, no tests at all might be even better. And I need to know where you are on your understanding of this material today. Plus, I want you to believe that when I announce a test I will follow through with that action. Nice try. Now get out your pencils and think positively."

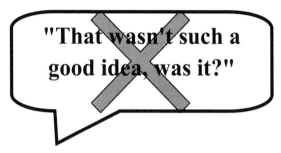

"That wasn't such a good idea, was it?"

Willie wrote in his language arts journal, "I put off working on my science fair project until the final weekend and then we had to go away." That comment was part of a three-paragraph reaction to the suggested topic of the day. His teacher chose to focus on the sentence by writing in the margin, "That wasn't such a good idea, was it?" In his next journal entry Willie wrote three sentences instead of three paragraphs.

Whether you're communicating with a student in person or through writing, listen nonjudgmentally. Nothing shuts off dialogue with a student faster than judgment. It ignores nurture and heads immediately to advice, teaching, or probing for further information.

To improve the quantity and quality of dialog, verbalization of understanding (nurture and empathy) must precede verbalization of teaching. "That must have been very frustrating. What was the result?" garners increased information. "I bet that was a shock. How did you handle it?" indicates listening and demonstrates understanding. It invites further dialog and is void of judgment.

"But when do I teach?" we're often asked by educators who take that important part of their responsibility seriously. Our answer: at any time the student is not caught in the midst of strong emotion, because if you try to teach under those circumstances, you're teaching someone who can't hear you.

The teaching voice can be used in a variety of ways throughout the school day for many different reasons. In the following chapter you will find the verbal skills that will help you do that effectively.

THE VOICE OF TEACHING

The teaching voice is used to explain how to multiply fractions, create contractions, and organize a science notebook. It focuses primarily on content, including learning how our system of government works, memorizing multiplication tables, and increasing skills involved in decoding words. Indeed, teachers are hired to help students learn basic skills, develop core competencies, and deliver the components of a standardized curriculum. That calls for teaching content. If you ignore that responsibility, you will probably not have your job for long.

The use of the teaching voice to deliver content is intended to help students become literate and competent in regard to material deemed important by local, state, or national decision makers. This is the voice that is expected to help students score well on state assessment tests and demonstrate that this place of learning is what some have narrowly defined as "a successful school."

While that use of the voice of teaching is necessary to demonstrate learning in a small range of chosen competencies, it is not the use we intend to concentrate on here. We assume you know how to teach children multiplication, English literature, and the life stages of a frog. After all, you studied for at least four years to become a professional educator. Our guess is you are using that part of the teaching voice effectively.

In this chapter we will explore another use of the voice of teaching—one that is equally, if not more, significant: the teaching of the silent curriculum. The silent curriculum is the curriculum that is not written down, the one that test makers do not see as important enough to include in their measures of school effectiveness. The silent curriculum is concerned with teaching to the whole child—his or her mind, body, and spirit.

It is a curriculum built not around subjects, but rather around core concepts such as honesty, diversity, responsibility, inner knowing, solution seeking, and personal power. It deals with teaching concepts that help students learn how to become successful human beings.

This use of the teaching voice is concerned with teaching students the interpersonal skills needed to do group work effectively. It is used to help students learn they can make decisions and find solutions. It shows them they can get what they need in order to do what they must. This voice teaches the relationship between cause and effect. It teaches that you can influence your own environment, and that to a great degree you are in charge of your own life.

The voice of teaching that we will talk about in this chapter teaches about personal responsibility, conflict resolution, and anger management. It focuses on letting students experience the importance of purpose, mission, and direction. It helps them learn to become self-motivated, self-disciplined, self-responsible, and self-controlled.

As we think about the value of this aspect of the teaching voice, we are reminded of the high school drama teacher who had some of his students perform at an annual regional board of education dinner.

The entertainment, provided by the hosting school's high school drama club, consisted of a short play acted by several juniors and seniors. A comedy, the play was intended to be light and lively, leaving the audience entertained and amused. It didn't work out that way.

The students performed flawlessly as the presentation began. Their timing was impeccable, and the audience roared at all the right moments. The students and all sixty-three board members seemed to be enjoying themselves.

Then it happened.

Suddenly, the young man who had the lead role paused in the center of the stage and took on a deer-in-the-headlights look that signaled he had forgotten his next line. He froze, and stared straight ahead. A prompt came from offstage. He began, but halted again, looking frightened. Another prompt came from the wings.

Everyone in the audience could hear the prompt. But for some reason, the student who stood center stage did not. He chose to bolt. He turned, walked off to his right, and disappeared. (Later it was discovered that he had walked out of the school, jumped in his car, and gone home.)

The crowd was visibly taken aback. They slumped in their chairs and let their mouths drop open. The drama instructor waited a few moments to see if the student would return. When he didn't, the instructor walked out on stage with the script in his hand and read the missing student's lines. The play continued with this drama teacher reading the necessary lines while the other students played out their roles.

The board members applauded at the end. The remaining performers took the customary curtain call and smiled at the appreciation and recognition they received. But when the curtain closed for the final time, the board members were left wondering what had happened to the young man. They sat in their seats whispering about the incident, their concern evident on their faces. That's when the instructor appeared from behind the curtain and began to speak.

"Some of you may be wondering about our lead actor and how he's doing," he began. "I don't know yet, but I can assure you that the end result will be positive. This incident has provided an opportunity for an incredible learning experience for everyone in the class, including me.

"What you saw was a young man stumble and fall. My job as a professional educator is to help him and the other students learn how to get back up from a fall. We will be working on this first thing tomorrow morning.

"Another responsibility of mine is to help young people learn to encourage and support others who have stumbled. This incident will provide me with the opportunity I need to teach that lesson. All of my students will get to practice this tomorrow.

"Please take no offense, members of the board, but although these important lessons are not covered in the textbooks you provide or measured on the tests students must take to determine their graduation eligibility, I believe they have great value.

"These are the lessons I live for as a teacher. This is where I feel I earn my money. I don't really teach drama, I teach human beings. So when one of my students makes a mistake like this, I rejoice. It gives me an exciting opportunity to help all of my students learn to become more effective human beings.

"It was a great night tonight. Tomorrow will be even better. Thanks for inviting us to present."

A long pause ensued.

It was followed by a standing ovation.

The professional educator in this story used the voice of teaching to teach county board of education members about the most valuable use of this voice.

More examples of how it works follow.

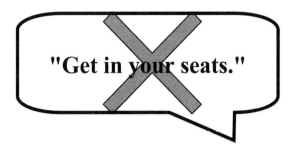

"Come in quietly."
"Hang your coats up."
"Get in your seats."
"Look at the board for the assignment."
"Take out your math books."
"Billy, turn around."
"Turn to page 56."
"Jason, read the first paragraph, please."
"Anita, pay attention."
"Brandon, read the second paragraph."
"Take out a pencil."
"Do the first problem on scrap paper."
"Stop talking."
"Keep working."
"Do your best."
"Pencils down."
"Eyes up here."
"Follow along as I explain the problem."
"Arwa, pay attention."

And on and on it goes in some classrooms, with the teacher issuing a seemingly endless stream of demands and students following them. Or not.

In these classrooms, students learn what school is like. They learn that school is an endless list of demands laid out by adults and that their job is to comply.

One big problem with commands is that sooner rather than later they activate the command-resistance cycle. The more you command, the more students resist, especially the students with power problems.

"I'm on page 61."

Use your teaching voice to give students information instead of commands. "I'm on page 61" resists the urge to tell your students what to do. Instead, it informs them of the page you are on and leaves it up to them to make an appropriate response. Use your Teacher Talk to teach your students that you believe they will make appropriate choices.

"Hang your coats up" is controlling. "Coats belong on hooks" is not. "The assignment is on the board" trusts that the students are smart enough to figure out a helpful next move. If Missy and Pablo begin whispering, notice the urge to say, "Stop talking." Instead, bite your tongue, reflect for a moment, and say, "Missy and Carlos, that's a side conversation. It is distracting. Please make a different choice."

"You will need a pencil for this" can take the place of "Get your pencils out." "Time is up" can be substituted for "Pencils down."

Over time, as you drastically reduce the number of commands that you utter, your students will become more empowered and begin to see themselves as more capable. As commands are reduced, so is student resistance. By changing your Teacher Talk you will be able to interrupt the command-resistance cycle in your classroom and add to the growth and maturity of your students. You will be teaching them to be more self-responsible and self-controlled.

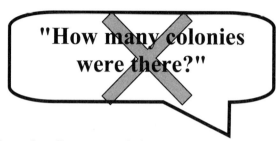

Before the first test of the school year, middle school students in a U.S. history class were expected to study for a test on the American colonies by designing possible test questions and having classmates answer them. The students went immediately to work when the teacher gave the signal to begin, and for the next ten minutes silently designed what they thought were appropriate test questions. At the end of that time, the teacher asked to hear some of the questions they had created. He heard:

"How many colonies were there?"

"What was the first colony?"

"Which colony did the Pilgrims found?"

"What year was the Virginia colony founded?"

"What colony did James Olglethorp lead?"

Every question created by the students was one that required a single right answer. Each was fact oriented. None asked for an opinion. None required thinking. All demanded a simple regurgitation of a fact. All relied only on the students' ability to memorize.

> # "Come up with a question that asks for higher-level thinking."

Hearing nothing but simple recall questions, the teacher challenged the eighth graders, "Come up with a question that asks for higher-level thinking."

"What's that?" one of the students asked.

"It's a question that asks for opinion, evaluation, or judgment," the teacher rattled off quickly, trying to think of a simple definition of higher-order questions.

"We haven't had any of those on tests, especially in a history class," another student informed him.

"Why not?"

"Because it's a history class," a third student responded.

"So?"

"History is about facts," the first student added. "There's no opinion to it."

"There's no opinion to history?"

"No, it's all facts. It either happened or it didn't," the student persisted.

"That doesn't exactly encourage you to think."

"There is no thinking to history. It's about facts. You just have to know them."

"Well, let's play with this for the rest of the hour," the surprised history teacher urged. "I'll suggest a certain type of question and you write one that fits the criteria I suggest. Write a question that begins with the words, 'What is your opinion about _____'," he challenged. After some initial resistance and grumbling, the students complied. Questions they designed included:

What is your opinion about why Plymouth was founded?

What is your opinion about the rules people had for living in the Massachusetts colony?

What is your opinion about the easiest colony to grow up in?

"Now give me a possible test question that begins with 'What factors led to _____'," the teacher instructed. Again he received questions that called for thinking and real understanding. In the remaining class time, he asked students to design questions such as:

1. Rank the _____ from best to worst on _____.
2. Sum up what you know about _____ in two sentences.
3. Predict what would have happened to _____ if _____.
4. Write a question that uses the words "same" or "different" and asks the person answering to compare or contrast something about the colonies.
5. What changes would you have made to_____? Why?
6. Evaluate how_____.
7. What in your own life is like _____ from _____.

By the time the class period ended, the eighth-graders were into the flow of asking questions that require thinking. It was no coincidence that by the end of the semester they were also competent at answering the same kind of questions—ones that require thinking.

> **"What is *one* good reason why?"**

The voice of teaching teaches students that their opinions are important and valued. This occurs when teachers actively and regularly use their teaching voice to invite student opinion. It matters less what opinions are asked for and more that they *are* asked for. It matters less what specific opinions are shared and more that teachers simply are there to acknowledge them without judgment.

When you seek student opinion, you communicate to students that their ideas have value, that you want and appreciate their input, and that their opinions are valid and useful. Opinion-seeking tasks help students see the value in their ideas as well as in themselves.

Opinion seeking is as simple as asking, "What do you think?" or "How do you feel about that?" It is as simple as purposefully designing inferential and hypothetical questions that have multiple right answers and inviting students to form opinions.

"What is *one* good reason why . . . ?" rather than "What is *the* reason why . . . ?"

Which of these pictures *might* be the home of a settler?" rather than "Which picture *is* the home of a settler?"

"Why *might* they have done that?" rather than "Why *did* they do that?"

"Who would be willing to read the paragraphs?"

One high school teacher uses file cards and his teaching voice to have students create what he calls "paragraph piles." Once a week he designs an opinion-seeking question and allows students five minutes to write a paragraph on a file card, stating their opinions.

He collects the completed cards and puts them in a pile on his desk. Two students then split the piles and alternately read the opinions expressed on the cards. No names are attached to the cards. A class discussion follows. Emphasis is on hearing and understanding the different opinions. There are no right or wrong answers. Not all opinions are agreed with. All opinions are respected.

"There will usually be four choices on a multiple-choice question. One or two of the answers you will know are not correct, so eliminate those and guess among the remaining options that seem possible to you."

Carmen Vasquez is a fourth-grader. She attends a quality school, one in which educators are proud of the high scores achieved by their students on state tests. Her school is continually near the top when the regional newspaper ranks area school districts according to test achievement and publishes their rankings. Carmen's parents are pleased and believe that all is well with the increased emphasis on testing and accountability.

Carmen is educated in a "progressive" school system, as described by the superintendant. The administrators and teachers take the testing program seriously. Grade-level goals and objectives are identified based on what is contained in the state tests. The tests drive the curriculum, and that curriculum is fiercely followed. What is on the test is what is taught. What is not on the test is essentially ignored.

Since the school leaders are invested in achieving high test scores, Carmen and her classmates receive much instruction in math, reading, and other basic skills that make up the crux of the state tests. In the weeks leading up to the all-important testing, much time is spent in test prepping. Teachers are expected to concentrate exclusively on the skills covered on the tests during those weeks.

Carmen and her peers also receive instruction on how to take tests. Recently, Carmen was taught how to answer multiple-choice questions. "If you know the answer, put it down," she was told by her teacher. "If you don't know the answer, make an educated guess."

An "educated guess" was explained this way: "There will usually be four choices on a multiple-choice question. One or two of the answers you will know are not correct, so eliminate those and guess among the remaining options that seem possible to you. In that way you will have more correct answers and create a better score for yourself." Her teacher and the others in that school did a thorough job helping students learn everything the teachers knew about the importance of tests and how to take them to achieve the best results possible.

On testing day, Carmen ate a healthy breakfast, as instructed by her teacher. She also made sure she had gotten a good night's sleep so she was well rested for the important test. She took the test seriously and was happy that she knew the answers to many of the questions.

That night, Mr. Vasquez asked his daughter how she thought she had done on the test. "Good," Carmen said, "but I didn't know the answer to five of the questions so I left them blank." Surprised by her answer, Mr. Vasquez inquired, "Why did you leave them blank? Why didn't you guess?" Her answer revealed an intelligence not measured by the latest test and a more advanced understanding of the true meaning of testing than that demonstrated by the adults at her school. "If I had guessed," she told her father, "I might have gotten some of them right. Then Mrs. Jacobs would have thought I knew the answer. I left them blank so she would know which ones I really knew and which ones I didn't. That way she could help me learn the ones I didn't know."

Apparently, Carmen has some insights that could help educators learn about the real value of testing. Too bad she's just a kid.

> "If you don't know the answer, make an educated guess."

"If you don't know the answer, make an educated guess" teaches. It teaches students that how well they score on the test has a greater value than having educators learn what you know and what you don't know. This way of teaching children to take tests is not in the best interest of the learner. It is in the best interest of the adults. It is not designed to help kids learn. It is designed to help the school look good to the community, the politicians, the voters, surrounding schools and the media. What matters most are high scores, not children.

"I think I'll get started correcting these papers. A fast start helps motivate me to keep going."

"I'm going to write a note to the principal. I want to share my appreciation with him for the assembly he arranged for us."

"When I get home tonight, I'm going to run this parent newsletter through my spell-check. It's important to me to have no errors in it."

The examples above are characteristic of a Teacher Talk technique known as "self-referred comments." Using self-referred comments such as these is one useful way to use your teaching voice to communicate values, ideals, and personal standards to your students.

To make a self-referred comment, structure the first part of your Teacher Talk so you are speaking about yourself. Follow your comment about yourself with a values connection.

"I think I'll organize my desk." (comment about self) "It's a lot easier to find things in an organized desk." (values connection)

"I'll pass on the cupcake, thanks." (comment about self) "I want nutritious foods fueling my engine." (values connection)

"I'm going to write that note to your mother right now." (comment about self) "I want to make sure I keep my word to your mother." (values connection)

To increase the chances that students will notice your positive modeling, use self-referred statements as you are performing the act you're talking about. Talking about what you're doing while you do it adds an auditory component to the visual one. If you're modeling getting started quickly, for example, say: "I think I'll get going on these right away. Getting a fast start gives me a better chance of finishing my work before I go home." Then give visual support to your Teacher Talk by following through with a quick start.

When you apologize to a student, the structure of your Teacher Talk is important. Just saying, "I'm sorry," is not enough. It does not teach. Telling someone you're sorry is an example of asking for cheap forgiveness. It requires no thinking on your part, no recognition of what needs to be altered, no plans for improvement. Just say you're sorry and move on. Nope. Not good enough. Instead, use your teaching voice to teach.

> **"I am aware that I listed the wrong assignment on the web site. I see the confusion it created. I'm sorry. I will double-check the listings for accuracy from now on."**

Model an effective apology by including what happened, the effect it had on others, what you learned, and what you will do differently next time. This style of speaking teaches. It teaches students that simply saying you're sorry is not good enough. It teaches them what you are now conscious of, what you have learned, and what your goal is for next time.

> **"I'm sorry I reprimanded you in front of the class, but your choice of behavior was inappropriate."**

If you yell, use sarcasm, or publicly ridicule a child, an apology is definitely appropriate. When apologizing, be careful how you use the word "but."

"I'm sorry I reprimanded you in front of the class, *but* your choice of behavior was inappropriate" uses "but" to excuse your own inappropriate behavior. Strengthen your apology by changing the order of your Teacher Talk. Say, "Your choice of behavior was inappropriate, but I'm sorry I reprimanded you in front of the class."

An even more effective apology occurs when you replace "but" with "and." Tell the student, "Your choice of behavior was inappropriate, *and* I'm sorry I reprimanded you in front of the class."

"We have a problem."

Shadid Kurubacaq noticed a problem surfacing in her fourth-grade classroom recently. Her students were misbehaving on their visits to the hall bathroom. "I noticed that certain class members were being silly, making loud noises, and getting each other wet in the bathroom," she told us. "I decided this problem needed to be solved and figured the best way to do that was to present it to the students. I called a class meeting, assuming we could find a solution together while giving my students one more experience with using a solution-seeking process."

> ## "I'm concerned
> ## that ... "

Shadid used a six-step process in dealing with her concern. Step one was sharing her own perceptions of the situation. "I'm concerned that some of you are not using your quiet voices in the bathroom," she began. "Also, some of you have not been respecting your classmates' space with regard to your hands or splashing with water. I'm concerned that someone could get hurt. In order for you all to say safe it's important to continue to respect one another when we're outside our classroom walls. In addition, we're disturbing children in nearby classrooms who are trying to study."

After sharing her perceptions, Shadid moved to step two and asked the students to share theirs. They agreed that disruptive behavior had been going on in the bathroom. Several students cited incidents that had occurred recently. A couple of them wanted to name specific people. "When in these solution-seeking sessions I prefer they tell me about behaviors and not about classmates," Shadid said. "I refocused them on the behaviors we were concerned with and the problem we were working to solve."

At this point, step three, she and the class redefined the problem and wrote the definition on the chalkboard. It stated, "Help all of us remember to be respectful in the bathrooms."

"I am not interested in blaming, only in finding a solution."

With the problem visible to all, Shadid moved to step four, brainstorming possible solutions."This is often a difficult part for them," she told us. "They want to blame and punish. The fourth-graders suggested that we have the guilty people lose their bathroom privileges and make the problem kids go alone. I told them I wasn't interested in blaming, only in finding a solution."

The teacher wrote their solutions on the board. The suggestions included: sending one person at a time to the bathroom; sending only a few; tapping the person being disrespectful on the shoulder and reminding them of appropriate behavior; having students take a checklist of bathroom rules with them and check off the ones they observed.

During step four Shadid often had to remind her students not to evaluate the suggestions. The emphasis at this step is on the quantity of ideas produced. The goal is to generate as many solutions as possible without evaluating them.

In step five the teacher and the class reached agreement on which one or combination of solutions they thought would work. They didn't talk about which ones were good or bad. They concentrated instead on what would work for them. In this case, students chose to go with tapping the person on the shoulder as a reminder if they were getting too loud or disrespecting someone's space. The students then role-played that solution in front of the class and debriefed the practice session.

Then, in step six, these fourth-graders made a commitment as a class by giving a quick thumbs-up if they were willing to use this solution. All thumbs were up. A date was set to evaluate the solution to see if it was working. That date was written on the board as a reminder of when they would get back together to evaluate their efforts. "If the solution solved the problem, we could invest a few minutes congratulating ourselves for finding a solution that worked," Shadid said. "We could feel powerful, part of a powerful group. Better than that, we would feel like a powerful solution-seeking group. If it didn't work, we would go back to the drawing board and create some more possible solutions. The lesson here is that we don't always solve the problem with the first attempt. And we never give up searching for solutions."

Shadid used her teaching voice to guide students through a solution-seeking process. She helped them learn . . .

- to see themselves as solution seekers.
- to search for solutions rather than fix blame and punishment.
- to use their own power in helpful ways.
- to engage in possibility thinking.
- to listen to others.
- to speak up for themselves.
- to self-evaluate.
- to work with others and be part of a group.

> ## "Act as if you can."

Five foot nine. Two hundred ten pounds. Clearly the prototype of the Pillsbury Doughboy.

That was Chick in high school. And it was that body, along with an equally unconditioned attitude, that he dragged to physical education class every day in 1959. Irv Menzel was the instructor. He was also the boys' basketball coach. He owned a whistle and a clipboard and what looked like one set of clothes which he appeared to wear every day.

Coach Menzel was determined in the winter semester of that year to have all students learn how to do, among other things, a neck spring. A neck spring, for those of you who aren't familiar with it, is a physical maneuver that begins with lying flat on your back on a mat. You then rock back and forth until you get as far up on your shoulders as possible. At that critical point, you place your hands behind your shoulders and plant them firmly on the mat. You then push with your hands, at the same time kicking your legs forward. If all goes as planned, you land on your feet.

Chick could not do a neck spring. He tried. He practiced. He was just too out of shape. Too many pounds, not enough muscle. Give him a middle linebacker to block and he was your man. Forget this neck spring thing. That was for gymnasts. He was a football player.

On testing day, Coach Menzel appeared with his clipboard and whistle. "On the mat, Moorman," he said, when it became Chick's time to demonstrate his ability. Chick complied.

"Give me a neck spring," the coach commanded.

"I've never done a neck spring," Chick whispered meekly.

"I didn't ask you if you had ever done one. I asked you to do one for me now."

"Coach, I can't do a neck spring."

"Moorman, *act as if* you can. *Act as if* you have done five of them already."

"But I haven't done any."

"I didn't ask you how many you have done. Just *act as if* you know how to do one."

"OK, Coach."

With adrenaline pumping and classmates watching, Chick rocked back and forth until he got high on his shoulders. Then he pushed and kicked simultaneously in a way he had never pushed and kicked before. For whatever combination of reasons, he landed on his feet. Barely. He had successfully completed the first neck spring of his life. The coach checked him off his list and called on another student.

Fifty-plus years later, Chick remembers that first neck spring. He is also aware that it is the *only* neck spring he has ever done. That's right. He has never used that skill anywhere, ever, in his entire life. Which prompts us to say that a neck spring is not unlike a lot of other things we learn in school that we will never use again in our entire lives. Which then leads us to wonder why teachers teach those things in the first place.

As Chick thinks back, reflecting on what Irv Menzel taught him many years ago, he's aware that the neck spring was not what the coach was really teaching. The neck spring was merely the water he was splashing around in. What he was actually teaching is that you can do anything you set your mind to—that you can do things that might seem impossible at first glance if you act as if you can—and that the power of belief in yourself is a mighty force if harnessed in a focused direction.

Yes, Irv Menzel was a physical education teacher. But he was much more than that. Quietly, without a lot of fanfare, he put spirit in the forefront of the important educational trilogy of mind, body, and spirit. He taught that you might not always be able to control what you can do, but you can always control how you stand in it, the attitude you bring to it, the energy you apply to it, the way you approach it, and how you talk to yourself about it.

> **"The words you use to talk to yourself are like seeds you plant in your mind."**

"If I don't pass this test, I'll be in trouble."

"If she calls on me, I won't know what to say."

"I'll never be able to find what I need in the library."

"If I don't get to sleep, I won't do well in the game tomorrow."

Isn't it just incredible how accurate students are at predicting their future? Perhaps you can use your teaching voice to help them make more positive, emotionally healthy predictions.

Do your students talk to themselves? Of course they do. Kindergartners talk to themselves. Fifth-graders talk to themselves. And high school students talk to themselves. In fact, all students talk to themselves, and they do it often.

Eighty percent of talk is self-talk. The remaining twenty percent is directed at others. Since all students talk to themselves, it seems it would be beneficial to help them become conscious of the nature of their self-talk and how it's affecting their school performance and their lives. It appears that in many schools teachers invest more time getting students to stop talking out loud than they do helping them examine how they talk to *themselves* when they are not talking out loud.

Self-talk is programming that affects students' minds. It is one of the major ways in which they create beliefs that influence their actions. When they tell themselves, "I probably won't like this new chapter," they are programming themselves for failure. If their inner dialogue is, "No one is going to like my speech," they are setting themselves up to do poorly.

As educators, wc often design lessons to teach students what to say when they are giving their speech. Rarely do we help them learn how to talk to themselves before, during, and after their speech.

Do you teach your students about the importance of self-talk? Do you tell them, "The words you use to talk to yourself are like seeds you plant in your mind"? Before a test, do you ask them to pay attention to what they are saying to themselves? Michael Olson does.

> ## "What did you tell yourself?"

The first time Michael Olson passed out a social studies test to his seventh-graders, he asked them to leave it face down on their desks for a few moments. Students were expecting that their teacher would soon be giving them the signal to turn it over and begin. They were in for a surprise.

"We are not going to take this test right now," this teacher informed his students. "We're going to do something else instead. I want you to pay attention to what you were telling yourself as the test was distributed. Get in touch with what you were saying to yourself. Were your thoughts positive or negative? I'll give you three minutes to write some of them on the back of your test paper."

After the three minutes had passed, Mr. Olson called time and asked students to share aloud some of the comments they wrote. Their contributions included:

"I should have studied more."

"This is not going to be pretty."

"I hope I get a good grade."

"I can do this."

"I don't want to do this."

"I don't like tests."

"I wonder if it will be hard."

Many students were surprised at how many negative messages they gave themselves. Some could not recall telling themselves anything at all.

As part of his lecture burst on this self-talk lesson, Mr. Olson told the students, "The words you use to talk to yourself are like seeds you plant in your mind. They sprout quickly, take root, and grow strong. Be careful what you plant in your mind. It will affect what you harvest in the future." Following his lecture and a discussion, students were challenged to think positive thoughts about the test.

Many times during the semester Mr. Olson stopped and asked students to examine their inner dialog. He challenged them to say positive thing to themselves with the following Teacher Talk.

"Where is the talk you are saying to yourself right now leading you?"

"Is your self-talk creating the kinds of beliefs you want to develop?"

"Is your self-talk helping or hurting what you are trying to accomplish?"

"What would you be saying to yourself if you were choosing your self-talk on purpose right now?"

> **"Write down all the negative comments you can think of about math."**

Patty Tamble teaches math to high school students in Minnesota. "I have a group of students in a low-ability class who make no secret of the fact that they hate math," she told us. "They inform me continually that they can't do math."

It was obvious to Patty that her students needed a new attitude toward math. Since they had accumulated years of negative experience with math and had developed strong core beliefs about the subject, Patty needed a strategy to help them start over. She needed an activity that would help them throw away their old beliefs about math and begin again, hopefully with a new attitude.

The idea that Patty came up was not found in a curriculum guide. It wasn't in her math textbook, either. The idea came from somewhere deep inside this Minnesota math teacher, the one who teaches students who don't like math.

One class period Patty asked her students to take out a blank piece of paper. They did. Then she asked them to write all the negative comments they could think of about math on their papers. They did.

With the first part of the assignment accomplished and her students' full attention, Patty continued to use her teaching voice.

> **"Now ball up your papers and crush them in your hands."**

"Crush all those negative beliefs about math," she challenged. "Take out every math frustration you have ever had on that balled-up piece of paper. Get into it. Squeeze it tight. Squeeze the irritation, the embarrassment, the fear right out of it." Once again, students followed her instructions.

"It's time now," she announced, "to throw away those old math attitudes, to begin again with a fresh attitude, with a clean slate. I want you to line up, beginning on my right, and throw your old math attitudes away. I want you to pitch them right here into the recycling bin." Row by row, student by student, they lined up, threw away their old math attitudes, smiled, and returned to their seats.

Patty knows that building new math attitudes with these students could be a long, slow process. She knows that developing positive attitudes toward math after years of frustration will require much dedication, persistence, and effort on her part. She's up to it. She has her teaching voice and she knows how to use it.

> # "Richard, that's an excuse. Excuses are not accepted in this classroom because . . ."

"My dad went bowling last night and my backpack is in his truck."

"She did it to me first."

"My mom forgot to sign it."

"The homework helpline didn't say it was due."

"Somebody must have taken it."

"It's not my fault that I'm late."

Excuses. There are as many excuses as there are students to use them. Some are new. Others are old and overused. Some are downright cute and clever. Yet they all have one thing in common. Students use them to excuse their failure to handle responsibility in a given situation.

Are you tired of student excuses? Do you wish they would go away? Do you want to end them in your classroom? Why not use your teaching voice and apply the One-Minute Behavior Modifier (explained in depth in our book, *The Only Three Discipline Strategies You Will Ever Need*, www.personalpowerpress.com) to the excuse-giving behavior of your students? That's what Sally Chapman, who teaches in a small town in Wisconsin, did with her eighth-grade special education students.

Sally is a veteran professional educator who has experienced the transition from self-contained classes to the inclusive model. She can see the pros and cons of both delivery systems. Regardless of the educational structure, her main concern remains the attitude of learned helplessness shown by many of her students. So Sally works hard to help her students see themselves as capable, skilled, and responsible. That's why she gets frustrated with excuses.

"My students are notorious for making excuses for any given situation," she says. "They blame others for the choices they made: late assignments, not getting to class on time, missing a detention, and so on." Fed up with excuses, Sally decided to take action. She created a One-Minute Behavior Modifier statement and planned to use it with her students every time she heard an excuse. This is the statement she created.

"Richard, that is an excuse. Excuses are not accepted in this classroom because if I accepted excuses I would be encouraging you to disown responsibility for the actions and choices you are making. What we do in this classroom instead of offering an excuse is accept responsibility for the choices we make by saying, 'I chose that behavior and I am responsible for the consequences.'"

Sally rehearsed the One-Minute Behavior Modifier and her new approach to making excuses before she put it into practice. When she went to class the next day, she was prepared and motivated.

It didn't take long for Sally to get an opportunity to put her new approach to use. During her second-hour class a student offered an excuse for being late. Sally responded calmly, "Sara, that is an excuse. I don't accept excuses in this classroom because if I accepted excuses I would be encouraging you to disown responsibility for the actions and choices you are making. What we do in this classroom instead of offering an excuse is accept responsibility for the choices we make by saying, 'I chose to be late and am responsible for the consequences.'"

The student looked at her teacher with a puzzled expression. She didn't know how to respond. Other students looked up, and the situation led to a discussion with the resource class about taking responsibility for your choices and actions.

Sally used the One-Minute Behavior Modifier several more times that week. "Several of my students gave me the deer-in-the-headlights look," she said. "They weren't quite sure how to react to my statement." Sally's new approach to excuse giving gave her students something to think about. Often they turned away, processing the information they had just received from their teacher. One student, after numerous attempts at making excuses, finally gave up and said, "All right, you caught me. Now what?" That led to another important class discussion on how we all like to get out of uncomfortable situations and the ways we attempt to do that.

Sally demonstrated over time that excuse giving wasn't going to work with her. Since students usually choose behaviors that work, her eighth-graders gradually reduced the frequency with which they offered excuses and took increased responsibility for their choices

"I'm pleased with how well they reacted to my new approach," Sally says. "And I'm pleased with myself for remembering to do it. I feel less stressed about the whole situation. With this new technique I don't feel drained trying to get them to face reality with one of my long lectures."

What Sally demonstrated is that changing negative behaviors in students does not have to be a time-consuming process. Implementing the One-Minute Behavior Modifier is a quick and effective way to reduce excuse giving in your classroom.

> "We're going to learn another responsibility skill today."

"It's not my job to teach responsibility. I am a math teacher. They should learn that stuff at home," a teacher told us recently. We occasionally hear variations on that same theme.

"They *should* already know how to get started quickly."

"Somebody *should* have taught them how to ignore distractions."

I *shouldn't* have to spend time teaching this. The parents *should* teach them how to disagree politely."

"They *should* have learned this in elementary school."

Agreed. Agreed. Agreed. Agreed. Agreed. We agree with you on every one of the comments above. Somebody *should* have. The problem is, nobody did. And what is, is.

Students frequently demonstrate a lack of understanding of even the most rudimentary of self-responsibility skills. You can complain all you want about that. You can make frustrated remarks in the teachers' lounge. You can protest loudly to your principal or whisper your concerns to a friend. None of that will change a thing. The only way to change students' ability to act more responsibly is to stop *shoulding* about it and use your teaching voice to help them learn some new behaviors. If you want a behavior, you have to teach a behavior. If you are not willing to teach it, you're not going to get it.

Following is only a partial list of self-responsibility skills you might have to teach this semester.

1. Staying on task
2. Completing things
3. Asking for help
4. Having your materials on hand
5. Getting started quickly
6. Ignoring distractions
7. Asking for makeup work
8. Sharing materials
9. Owning your behaviors
10. Speaking up if you don't understand
11. Attending physically and mentally
12. Showing respect to the guest teacher
13. Checking your work
14. Disagreeing politely
15. Lining up appropriately
16. Reacting to winning/losing
17. Reading and reacting to written comments

18. Exhibiting sportsmanship

19. Reacting to a classmate's mistake

Once again, if you want a behavior, you need to teach a behavior. If your students show a need to learn these or any similar responsibility skills, we recommend that you use your teaching voice to engage in direct teaching or build a T-chart as described later in this chapter.

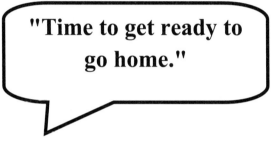

"Time to get ready to go home."

"Some of my students were not preparing themselves well to go home," a middle school teacher told us. "Some would forget to take home important materials they would need to prepare for the next school day."

This educator decided to discontinue using her teaching voice to complain, remind, or give lectures to students concerning their behaviors. She chose instead to teach her students exactly how to get ready to go home by using the direct teaching method that we advocate.

With the direct teaching method you pick a behavior and teach it directly to students by presenting three to five clearly stated instructions. Keep it simple. Six or more steps can hamper the learning process. When teaching very young children, use only three steps and keep the words and phrases short. Add pictures if possible.

In teaching her students how to get ready to go home, this middle school teacher listed four items on a chart.

1. Compare the assignment board with your assignment notebook to make sure you have all the necessary material written in it.
2. Get out the materials you will need to properly complete your homework/studying, and put them in your backpack/bag.
3. Clean up your workspace (desk and floor).
4. Ask the teacher any questions or state any concerns you have about your homework before you leave.

This middle school teacher invested fifteen minutes that day to teach her students how to prepare to go home. After she told them why she was teaching this particular piece, she wrote one item at a time on a chart as she explained it. When all four items had been added, she hung the chart on the wall and invited students to copy it into their Responsibility Notebooks.

On that first day the teacher walked her students through the four steps one at a time while they implemented the suggestions. For the next two days students practiced following the written procedure on their own, with the teacher debriefing their efforts. Improvement was immediate and dramatic. In the debriefing, the class discussed why they thought the *prepare to go home* procedures had improved, and each student recorded in his or her Responsibility Notebook improvements he or she planned to make next time.

After a few days of debriefing, students were left on their own to implement the process. The use of the direct teaching method in dealing with this problem reduced it greatly. Thanks to this teacher, her students now had a procedure to follow and the skills necessary to behave self-responsibly when getting ready to go home.

"Are you on
TOPIC?"

Patty Tamble, a teacher you met earlier in this chapter, believes that time on task is strongly related to learning. Like many tenth- to twelfth-graders, her students are not always on task. "I have some students," she says, "who waste their time and disrupt others rather than work on problems."

Patty set out to correct that situation. Believing that if you want a behavior you have to teach a behavior, she decided to teach her students how to "be on topic." She chose to use the direct teaching approach by detailing five behaviors that are necessary to do this. She wrote each behavior on a white board as she explained and talked about it. As she wrote the five items, she made the first letter of each word in each item extra large, spelling the word "TOPIC."

1. **T**urn to the proper page.
2. **O**pen your notebook.
3. **P**ick up your pencil.
4. **I**nfo in upper-left-hand corner.
5. **C**oncentrate on your work.

Near the end of each of her classes, Patty debriefed with her students by asking them to rate themselves on a scale of one to ten on how well they had been on topic that day. She also assigned students the task of completing the sentence starter, "Next time, we can be on topic better if we . . ." A brief discussion followed. (More on debriefing in chapter five.)

"The five steps are clear and easy for my students to remember with the help of the poster," Patty reported. She added, "It also helped to give the preferred behavior a name. Asking 'Are you on TOPIC?' has replaced giving students reminders such as 'Pick up your pencil and get to work.' Since I invested the time in teaching the behavior I wanted, my students have been on task a lot more often."

> **"OK, get back to your seats. Put the microscopes away. No more responsibility for you until you can show me you know how to be responsible."**

Teachers often respond to mistakes involving responsibility, cooperation, and respect by taking related opportunities away from students. "OK. No more working in groups until you show me you can handle it."

If you apply that same logic to math, it would sound like this: "OK, no more long division for you until you can show me you can do long division." Obviously, that makes no sense. If students make mistakes in math, we give them more math. They get reteaching during the lunch period. They get a tutor for the weekend.

Treat mistakes in responsibility the same way you treat mistakes in the content areas. If students make mistakes in responsibility, use your teaching voice to reteach. That's what Shingo Matsousaka does.

> ## "Let me show you how we put the microscopes away."

Shingo Matsousaka watched his middle school students closely as they returned microscopes to the shelf following an activity. Some carried them gently across the room, as if they were handling a baby. Others did not. Some placed them on the shelf without looking at the other microscopes that were already there. Others did not. Some did it quickly and roughly. Others did not. Two students banged microscopes together as they vied for the same spot on the shelf. Shingo knew then that it was time to activate his teaching voice. He chose to do that using the T-chart method of instruction.

This five-year teaching veteran began class the next day with the words, "Let me show you how we put the microscopes away." With all eyes on him, he demonstrated the desired method of returning the valuable and fragile equipment. Then he addressed the class.

> # "Tell me what it looks like to . . ."

"We're going to build a T-chart," Shingo informed his students. At the top of a blank piece of chart paper he wrote, "Returning Microscopes Safely." Underneath those words he drew a large T. On the left side of the chart he wrote the words, "Looks Like." "You saw me put away the microscope," he told his students. "Tell me what you saw. What did it *look like?*" Through his Teacher Talk, he induced responses from his students that required inductive thinking. On the chart, he recorded their responses, which included:

- Be gentle.
- Walk slowly.
- Watch where you walk.
- Hold the microscope with two hands in front of you.
- Put it slowly and carefully on the shelf.

He then wrote the words, "Sounds Like" on the right side of the T-chart and asked, "What did you hear?" Students responded with:

- Quiet
- Soft footsteps
- No bumping of microscopes

With the T-chart specifying what returning microscopes safely looked like and sounded like, Shingo invited lab partners to select one person from each pair to get a microscope. Then he asked the other person to return it. After practicing getting and returning microscopes several times, he had students copy the material from the T-chart, adding it to their Responsibility Notebooks.

"Let me tell you what I noticed when you used microscopes yesterday."

How did Shingo know that his students needed direction on how to return a microscope carefully? And why did he teach that specific skill? The answer is that he's a skilled professional educator who knows how to use two powerful tools: *diagnosis and prescription.*

The first step is to diagnose. This is done through basic observation. This teacher noticed that his students were misusing the microscopes. If he hadn't observed any mistreatment, he would not have picked that skill for teaching.

In the medical model, prescription without diagnosis has a name. It's called malpractice. If your elbow hurts and the doctor wraps your knee, it might not hurt your knee, but it will not help your elbow. The same holds true in the field of education. If a child is struggling with how to show respect for the guest speaker and we teach him how to respect the microscope, it probably won't help him much when another guest speaker appears on the scene.

Build a T-chart on how to get started quickly if you notice students taking a long time to begin. Teach how to invite others to participate only if you notice "hitchhikers" sitting doing nothing in their groups. Teach how to ignore distractions if students' attention is being diverted by the construction going on next door.

Invite students to add all of the T-charts to their Responsibility Notebooks, where they will be readily available when needed for review. How do you know when it's time to review? Through diagnosis and prescription.

> **"Help me collect what it looks like and sounds like."**

Students who find substitute teachers replacing their "real" teacher for a day do not always treat the substitute with the respect he or she deserves. The appearance of a sub is often the signal for students to engage in a series of behaviors they would typically not choose if the regular classroom teacher were present. Sitting in different seats, answering to different names, initiating power struggles, refusing to follow directions, ignoring directions, talking more and working less are just a few of the antics that some students choose to engage in the presence of a substitute teacher.

Part of the problem can be traced to the word *substitute*. The prefix *sub* often indicates inferior, not as good as, or next best. If you played *subpar,* you played below average. A *substandard* performance points to one that was below your usual standard. When the advertised special is sold out, you are often offered a *substitute.* When a star player is injured, the coach puts in a *substitute.* That being the case, it's not surprising that students learn to view a *sub*stitute teacher as being a level or two below their regular teacher.

That's why Laurie Tandrup, a fifth-grade teacher at an elementary school in Alberta, Canada, doesn't have a substitute teacher when she's ill or goes to a professional meeting. Instead, when she is absent, the fifth-graders have a *guest* teacher. And Laurie's students have been taught to treat a guest teacher like they would be expected to treat any other guest—with respect.

Laurie believes that if you want a behavior you have to teach a behavior. So the last time she knew in advance that she was going to be absent, she prepared her nine- and ten-year-olds for the event. Laurie began her preparations the day before she would be gone. She invited students to help brainstorm a list of what it would *look like* and *sound like* to respect the guest teacher. Students decided that respect in this case would *look like* following directions, sitting in your seat, working on assignments, finishing work, and raising hands to ask and answer questions. Their list of *sounds like* behaviors included one person talking at a time, asking for help if needed, asking for permission to do things, and saying please and thank you. The class practiced the behaviors for a portion of the day. Debriefing followed, feedback was given and the list adjusted slightly.

> ## "Help me plan the day tomorrow."

Next, Laurie enlisted her students' input in planning the day. They took each subject (math, language arts, physical education, etc.) and planned what they wanted to have happen while the guest teacher was there. The lessons had to fit Laurie's criteria of being related, rigorous, and relevant. The criteria were satisfied as students decided to use computers to do research for an essay during language arts time, make corrections and skill-practice for math, and do warm-up running and skill challenges for physical education. By involving students in crafting their own day, Laurie built ownership for the design of the day. She empowered her students, creating less need for them to exercise power at the expense of the guest teacher.

> ## "How will we know if we've been successful?"

Finally, this second-year teacher asked students to come up with a list of criteria they could use to tell if the day they designed turned out to be an excellent day, a good day, an average day, or a day that needed much improvement.

Students, with her help, created behavioral descriptors for each level.

Laurie left a detailed note for the guest teacher to let him know what to expect. She then designed a few debriefing questions that she would use with the class when she returned after the guest teacher had been there. Her brief list included:

1. Rate on a scale of 1-10 the degree to which you respected the guest teacher. Explain your rating by telling why you chose that number.

2. What is one thing you did to respect the guest teacher yesterday? Why do you think that thing was important?

3. What is one improvement you feel our class could make next time to show increased respect for the guest teacher?

The morning of her return to the classroom Laurie placed the debriefing questions on the board. Students were asked to write their reactions on paper. A lively discussion followed. The processing of the previous day's experience helped students look at their behaviors and learn from them.

All of Laurie's students helped design, create, and evaluate their day. All had an experience with assessing their own behavior. All had an opportunity to think critically about the behaviors they chose. All had an experience with learning how to show respect for a guest teacher.

> ## "What are you trying to accomplish?"

"What do you want it to look like when you get done?"
"What would you be happy with?"
"What are you aiming for?"
"What is the exact outcome you want?"
"What are you creating?"

Use the Teacher Talk above to help your students create mental models of what they are working toward. Asking questions of this nature helps them create vision, mission, and detailed purpose in their minds. It teaches them to be goal oriented and focused.

> ## "Compare this paper to the one you did earlier."

Grandma lives in Arizona. Her grandkids live in Illinois. So every time Grandma sees them, which is usually once a year, she exclaims, "My, have you grown. Just look at how tall you are."

Growth of her grandchildren appears to Grandma as a big spurt. The parents and the children don't see their growth the same way. Parents see their children every day and therefore don't see the physical growth as a spurt at all. The children look in the mirror and see no change from day to day. Because parents and children are together frequently, they don't see growth through grandmothers' eyes. They're too close to the situation to be conscious of the dramatic change that is gradually taking place.

Cathy Smithson, a fifth-grade teacher from the Midwest, understands the concept of grandmothers' eyes. She also understands its importance. So this past school year she used her teaching voice to give her students several opportunities to see themselves with grandmothers' eyes.

She began by collecting several examples of each student's penmanship at the beginning of the year. She placed them in a portfolio for each student. She added to the collection her students' early papers showing their efforts with long division. Also included was a pretest on social studies chapter terms, an audio recording of each student reading, and various other examples of early fifth-grade work.

At the end of the school year, Cathy assigned a penmanship lesson. At the conclusion of the activity she produced the early penmanship samples she had saved, passed them out to each student, and asked her students to compare them. The fifth-graders were stunned. Comments they made included:

"I used to write like a baby."

"I'm so much neater now."

"I can hardly read what I wrote before."

"I sure have improved."

Cathy's students were beginning to see their progress through grandmothers' eyes. And she was only beginning.

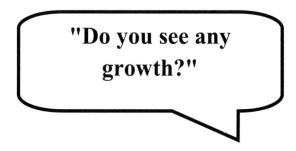

"Do you see any growth?"

Two days later she had students complete a long-division assignment. To all of them it appeared easy. She then produced the paper with the same assignment that they had done several months prior. Then she asked, "Do you see any growth?"

Their reactions?

"I used to think this was so hard."

"The first time I got half of them wrong."

"I get it now."

"Boy, did I learn a lot this year!"

Cathy followed the same procedure with the other items in the student portfolios. When they read a passage from their reading material and then heard themselves reading the same material earlier in the year, the experience was dramatic. "Some of them listened with their mouths open," Cathy reported. "I could see the surprised looks on their faces. The improvement they had made in a year was obvious to them. They were all smiling and looking proud."

Cathy Smithson showed students exactly what they had learned and how much they had grown academically. She provided visual and auditory proof of their achievements. By giving them end-of-the-year experiences of seeing with grandmothers' eyes, she helped them leave fifth grade feeling tall in their own eyes.

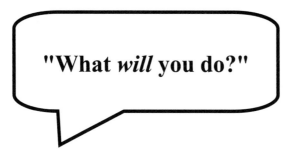

"I won't bug him anymore."

"I won't be late again."

"I won't blurt out the answer next time."

Each of the statements above represents a student's honest desire to change an undesirable behavior. Teachers can help turn these positive *intentions* into positive *actions* by using Teacher Talk that invites students to think about and articulate alternative behaviors.

Ask them, "What *will* you do?" This verbal skill moves students' thinking from what they will not do (hitting, being late, blurting out in class) to what they *will* do instead.

"What *will* you do?" is an invitation to students to articulate a plan of action that focuses on the positive. By stating that plan out loud, students strengthen their commitment and are more likely to put their plan into action. Your teaching voice helps students learn an appropriate alternative behavior.

> ## "Thank you for sharing your feelings with me."

What did you say this week that increased your students' emotional intelligence? Did your teaching voice help them learn about this valuable form of intelligence? Did it help them develop the skill of recognizing feelings, giving them a name, and handling them effectively?

"Tell me what you're feeling and what you attribute it to."

"You seem irritated."

"Are you mad (sad, glad, scared)?"

"Did you recognize the feeling at the time?"

"Let me teach you a positive way to manage anger."

"Sounds like you chose to be frustrated with that."

"What thought preceded that feeling?"

"I have a strange feeling in my gut. I think it's annoyance. Yep, I'm annoyed all right."

Talking about, reporting, inquiring about, naming, and discussing feelings builds students' emotional intelligence. This often neglected source of information and knowing is not present in many curriculum guides. Likewise, it is not measured by many of the popular tests being administered these days. Learning about emotional intelligence is a hole in a child's education that results from the continued narrowing of the curriculum, as we are witnessing going on today. Your teaching voice can help fill that hole.

> ## "I'm feeling apprehensive about this."

Students often reveal their limited vocabularies when they attempt to verbalize their feelings. Ask a student how she's feeling and you're likely to hear, "OK," "Fine," or "Bad." This three-word range for describing feelings can be attributed to two factors: first, children are not always in touch with their feelings; and second, even when they are aware of their feelings they lack the words necessary to describe them accurately.

To help students recognize, name, and talk about their feelings, add a variety of feeling words to your Teacher Talk.

"Sounds like you're feeling frustrated."

"Seems like you're furious with her."

"I can see the aggravation on your face."

"Exasperation is what I'm feeling right now."

"Looks like sadness to me."

"You seem dejected."

By using an expanded vocabulary of feeling words yourself, you help students identify and articulate their own feelings as well as increase their vocabulary of feeling words.

> ## "There is no such thing as luck."

"I guess it wasn't in the cards," one of Sean Tucker's seventh-graders announced after hoping for an A and not receiving it on a vocabulary test. Mr. Tucker used that occasion to abandon his scheduled lesson on dangling participles and teach instead about the many words and phrases in our language that refer to the concept of *luck*. He began his remarks with the words, "There is no such thing as luck."

He talked to his students that day about the results of assigning responsibility to fate or fortune when things do or do not go well. "You can assign the results that show up in your life to *fate or luck*, or you can *take the responsibility yourself* instead," he told them. "Where you place the responsibility goes a long way in determining what you can and will do about the situation. If you talk as if you are responsible and see where you are responsible, you are more likely to take responsibility for doing something about it. If you assign the results to *luck*, you tend to see yourself as someone who cannot affect the results. The choice of how to see these situations is yours."

During the year, Sean heard other students disowning responsibility for the results they produced. "I didn't have any *luck* with him at all," one student said after an unsuccessful attempt to talk another student into loaning him a pencil. Other examples of disowned responsibility he heard included:

"*Unfortunately*, everything went wrong with my presentation."

"I just *fell into it*."

"I *stumbled into it* in the library."

"It *came my way* as I was sitting there thinking."

In each case, this second-year teacher stopped his planned lesson and pointed out the use of the language of luck. His efforts helped his students become conscious of using this style of language and the effect it was having in their lives.

Sean Tucker is aware that the language of luck is not an item in his sixth- or seventh-grade curriculum guides. He knows that it is not one of the concepts tested on the state assessment instruments he is expected to administer each year. Yet, he never wavers in his insistence on helping his students appreciate the importance of this important language concept.

"I am a language arts teacher," he says with great pride and emotion. "I'm expected to teach the parts of speech, how to diagram sentences, and how to construct a meaningful paragraph, among other things. Those are all important mechanics for children to learn. And I do a good job teaching the mechanics of English. But I'm more than a mechanic. I am an artist. My job is also to teach the art of language. And I do that equally well."

To say that his students are *lucky* to have him as a teacher would not be appropriate here, would it? Let's just say we hope that Sean Tucker's students are alert enough to appreciate and recognize the important contribution this teacher is making to their understanding of the power of words and the importance of language.

> ## "What do you attribute that to?

Attribute awareness is an attempt to help students link their successes and failures to their own efforts. The goal is to have them attribute personal success to effort, energy, persistence or another factor over which they have control.

Attributions are the reasons that one assigns for achieving success or failure. Lack of ability, luck, insufficient effort, and difficulty of the task are the attributions most often used by students.

Using your teaching voice to structure your classroom so that students experience success is an important first step in helping them see themselves as successful. Another, more important, step occurs when a student realizes that she or he personally contributed to that success. Students must see the cause and effect connection between their behavior and the outcome they achieved in order to get the maximum benefit from their success. That's where the importance of effective Teacher Talk comes in.

Skillful Teacher Talk on your part can help students link effort, strategies, and ability with results. Some examples follow:

"Madison, this is your highest test score. I guess that extra practice had an effect."

"Latrell, that final revision put you over the top. It shows you really have learned to write in complete sentences."

"Pablo, your test score went up again. Using note cards seems to work for you as a study aid."

"Brenda, choosing not to complete the makeup assignments hurt your grade this time."

"I see your handwriting is becoming more legible. What do you attribute that to?"

Often students don't know why they failed or succeeded. When teachers use Teacher Talk like that in the examples above to give performance feedback that allows students to link results with effort, strategy, or ability, it helps them take responsibility in the present and raise expectations for the future.

> **"I just want you to do it to see if you can."**

Jason Lane, a brand-new sixth-grade teacher, could barely sleep the night before his first day at Riverdale Middle School. Four years of college, summers spent doing camp counseling, an exhaustive interview process, and a change of residence had brought Jason to this point. Now he was finally ready to face what he hoped would be eager eleven- and twelve-year-olds.

Although Jason had graduated from a prestigious Midwestern university with honors, earned an A in his student teaching, and gained valuable experience working with adolescents during his time as a camp counselor, nothing had prepared him for what he was about to encounter on this first day as a full-time professional educator.

Twenty-five youngsters greeted Jason Lane that first hour of his first day. He introduced himself, talked of his love for mathematics, explained that he believed mistakes were valuable learning tools and that he would challenge his students to make mistakes and learn from them. He distributed the textbook, talked about making math come alive as a useful concept in their lives, and shared some strategies for overcoming math anxiety. Jason then invited his students to turn to page two of the text, demonstrated the lesson on the chalkboard, and gave his first assignment.

That's when it happened.

"What do we get?" one of his students asked.

"What do you mean?" Jason queried the student.

"What do we get when we get it done?"

Not understanding the intent of the question, Jason said, "Say some more. I don't understand what you're asking."

Another student came to the rescue, informing the rookie teacher, "Usually we get something. Do we get points, a sticker, a grade, a smiley face? What's our reward?"

"How about M&Ms?" one student joked. Everyone laughed, including the teacher.

"I have nothing like that," Jason told his class. "I just want you to do it to see if you can."

> **"Because it feels good on the inside when you accomplish something."**

"If we don't get anything, then why should we do it?" asked a third student, new to the conversation.

"Because it's fun," Jason informed the class.

"Yeah, but what do we get?" another student pressed.

Somewhat flustered, Jason reached down deep and pulled out a response he had not been taught in college or even thought about previously. "What you get is . . . you get to feel good when you accomplish it."

"What does that mean?" another student asked.

"It means you get that inside feeling of accomplishment. You get to feel good that you did something. It's an inside thing that helps you feel good all over. It's better than points, grades, or stickers."

"I'd rather have points," said the student who had begun the discussion.

"Me too," added several others.

Just then the bell rang and the students quickly gathered up their belongings and exited the classroom, leaving their teacher rattled and bewildered.

"If you read fifty books, you can have a pizza party."

Jason Lane had not been prepared to deal with this unexpected situation. His students, on the other hand, had been prepared well. These youngsters had been prepared by their kindergarten teacher, who gave weekly homework assignments to five-year-olds and let them choose a prize if they turned it in on Friday. They had been prepared by their first-grade teacher, who, if they had been good, placed stickers on their hands as they exited the room at the end of the day. They had been prepared by their second-grade teacher, who occasionally placed M&Ms on the corner of their desks if they were working quietly. They had been prepared by their third-grade teacher, who gave a balloon to any student who read ten books. They had been prepared by their fourth-grade teacher, who placed gold stars at the top of all the spelling papers that were 100 percent correct. They had been prepared by their fifth-grade teacher, who held a pizza party to reward those who behaved well for three days when a substitute teacher was in charge.

Jason Lane's students had been prepared by well-intentioned teachers who had not understood the long-term effects of their reliance on rewards. They had been prepared by caring educators who did not comprehend that the negative effects of their actions do not appear immediately and who leave others to deal later with those negative effects. They had been prepared by teachers who took the quick and easy way out.

These youngsters had been prepared by a well-intentioned kindergarten teacher who did not know that she was using her teaching voice to teach children that school work is so distasteful we have to give them a prize so they'll want to do it. They had been prepared by a well-intentioned first-grade teacher who did not know that by offering a sticker for good behavior she was setting a precedent that required others who followed her to keep offering the same or larger bribes to gain compliance. They had been prepared by the well-intentioned second-grade teacher who did not know she was discouraging the use of internal reward systems by using one that was external. They had been prepared by a well-intentioned third-grade teacher who did not know that giving balloons to students for reading books was teaching them the reason we read is to earn an extrinsic reward and that those students may read less once the reward was withdrawn. They had been prepared by a well-intentioned fourth-grade teacher who did not realize that the more gold stars are awarded, the more they will be needed. They had been prepared by a well-intentioned fifth-grade teacher who had not yet realized that the more he got students to respond to pizza and similar rewards, the more they would require goodies in the future to motivate learning.

Jason Lane had a rough first day of school. He had not been as well prepared by his teachers as his students had been by theirs.

"Good!"

"Good job!"

"Bill does good work in science."

"She's making a good effort."

"Good way to do that!"

"It sure was a good choice!"

Recently we found a chart entitled "100 Ways to Say Good" hanging in a teachers' workroom. We were happy to discover that chart because for some time now we have been distressed by hearing adults tell children, "Good job." Our happy state didn't stay with us long, however, as we perused the list of synonyms prepared by a textbook company consultant.

"Great, Fantastic, Terrific, Marvelous, Splendid, Dynamic, Magnificent, Nifty, Supreme, First Rate, Sterling, Wonderful, Superb, Stupendous," and even "Foxy," filled the chart. And so it went: 100 examples of evaluative praise displayed in full color.

All was clearly not good with "good" or its synonyms. It's not that "Good job" is the worst thing you can say to students. It's just that there are so many more healthy, affirming, uplifting and even educational ways to praise them.

The first problem with evaluative praise is that it does not teach. It evaluates. It evaluates you, your product, your effort, your energy, your attitude, and even your being.

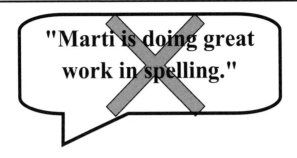

Imagine reading your daughter's report card. "Marti is doing great work in spelling. She has a good attitude. She is doing a good job in Social Studies."

As you read the report card, you quickly realize it doesn't tell you much about your daughter or her work in school. Good in spelling? What does that mean? You have no useful information about her accomplishments or her problems. You don't know if she learned anything or if she was good to start with. All you know is that one person evaluated her as "good." Compared to what? Or to whom? What does "good" mean? You just don't know.

Perhaps your son brought home a reaction paper with teacher remarks at the top. The teacher's comments were, "Good work. You did a nice job on this." You don't know what was good about it. You don't know what was nice about it. Your son doesn't know what to reproduce next time to merit another "good." The only thing the teacher's comments taught you and your son is that this teacher values his role as evaluator more than his role as teacher.

The "greats," "fantastics," "outstandings," and other synonyms don't do any more good than "good." They give no data. They simply label and evaluate.

Sitting on the front porch at a friend's house in the late afternoon recently, Chick was privileged to be part of an interesting educational exchange. As he and his friend caught up on the significant events in their respective lives, a school bus pulled up in front of his friend's house. Her two daughters descended the school bus stairs and began the walk from the road to the house.

As the girls approached the house, the older one, a tenth-grader, began waving a paper and calling excitedly to her mother. "Look what I got!" she cried. "An award from my writing teacher! It says I have an outstanding attitude!"

Chick's friend made appropriate congratulatory remarks as the award was passed to others for examination. Sure enough, Mindy had been presented with an 8 x10 suitable-for-framing award. It displayed these words: "Presented to Mindy Clark on March 21, 2011, for OUTSTANDING ATTITUDE in Creative Writing class." It was signed by the teacher.

Both mom and daughter were quite pleased with the written confirmation. That's when Chick stuck his nose in. He's been known to do that on occasion.

"What did you get that for, Mindy?" he asked.

"Having an outstanding attitude," she replied.

"So what exactly is 'an outstanding attitude'?" he pressed.

"It means I have a good attitude in writing class."

"What was good about your attitude?"

"What do you mean?"

"I realize that your teacher thinks you have an outstanding attitude, and I assume you probably do. But what I want to know is, what do you have to do to get that award?"

"You have to have an outstanding attitude."

"How does someone know if you have an outstanding attitude or not?"

"I don't know what you mean."

"Mindy, what if one of your girlfriends came up to you and asked what she would have to do, what behaviors she would have to demonstrate, to win that award next month? What would you tell her to do?"

"I'd tell her to have an outstanding attitude, a really good attitude, every day."

Chick soon realized that Mindy, age fifteen and an honor roll student, had no idea why she had received the award. She didn't know what behaviors of hers had produced it. She didn't know what behaviors to repeat to earn another outstanding attitude award.

Evaluative praise simply does not teach.

> **"I'll be passing out the Good-Student Awards now."**

Happy Grams, Good-Student Awards, and Superstar papers are handed out to students by well-intentioned teachers throughout the grades: in kindergarten, in fourth grade, and in high school. Regardless of the grade level, the awards have little meaning.

Awards that contain words like "excellent," "super," "tremendous," "fantastic," and "good" are one teacher's evaluation of a student in a given area. These and other similar words provide students with little useful data as to why they received the awards. In fact, when awards use evaluative language, students are more likely to consider their teachers as being responsible for creating the awards than to view themselves as having inspired them by demonstrating specific behaviors.

We have no doubt that Mindy has an outstanding attitude in her writing class. We also have no doubt that her teacher's evaluation was based on specific behaviors. We suspect Mindy turned her papers in on time, frequently participated in class discussions, asked questions, stayed on task, did in-depth work, and followed directions. No mention of any of those descriptors was on the award. The teacher missed an important opportunity to use her teaching voice.

"The statistics you included pointed the reader right to your conclusion."

When you give awards or comment on students' work or behaviors, strengthen your praise by adding descriptive comments. What was good about the paper? Why was the report fantastic? What behaviors made the effort super? Describe it.

"All your letters were right between the lines."

"That beginning sentence grabbed my attention and I wanted to read on."

"You moved the man in front of you back two feet and held your block for four more seconds."

"Yes! You did it. You spelled it correctly."

If you give a student an award for honesty, dependability, or promptness, go on to describe what it was he or she did that was honest, dependable, or prompt. By specifically describing accomplishments, you affirm what has been done rather than evaluate it. You allow students to draw their own conclusions. You give them room to make self-evaluations, and you help them connect their behaviors to the accolades they've received.

> **"Bill, I noticed you ignored Carlos's teasing and immediately returned to work."**

Positive behavior needs to be reinforced. An alternative to evaluative praise is the Character Support Statement. This important piece of Teacher Talk consists of two elements: a descriptive comment and a character connection. Examples follow:

"Bill, I noticed you ignored Carlos's teasing and returned to work." (descriptive comment) "When you do that, you demonstrate self-control." (character connection)

"Marlene, you have revised this report five times." (descriptive comment) "This shows determination and persistence on your part." (character connection)

"I see, Latrell, that you shared the blocks with Latisha." (descriptive comment) "You're learning about cooperation." (character connection)

By using Character Support Statements instead of evaluative praise, you leave room for the student to draw the conclusion. That allows the evaluation to come from the inside out rather than taking it from the outside and attempting to put it inside. Character Support Statements affirm what has been done and reveal the character connection so students can see the link between their behavior and their developing characters. When you use Character Support Statements you are implementing your teaching voice.

> **"Thank you for cleaning up the paint brushes before you left yesterday. You saved me fifteen minutes."**

Another style of praise that teaches is appreciative praise. Appreciative praise expresses gratitude and tells the effect the student's behavior had on your life and on the classroom.

"I appreciate you all getting your reports in on time." (appreciative praise) "That prevents me from having to go back and add other scores to my grade book later." (effect it had on your life)

"Thank you for treating the guest teacher with respect, as we've defined it on our T-chart." (appreciative) "That gives our whole class a positive reputation." (effect it had on the class)

"You really helped save my voice and reduce the strain on it." (effect it had on you) "I appreciate you using the bell to get kids to come in from recess." (appreciative praise)

Like descriptive praise, appreciative praise leaves room for the student to make the evaluation. If your words are, "Thank you for cleaning up the paint brushes before you left yesterday. You saved me fifteen minutes," then his self-talk can be, "I did a good job," or "I'm a good helper." The evaluation comes from him as opposed to being imposed on him by an outside source. Students are less likely to dismiss comments that are self-generated than they are comments that come from others.

Appreciative praise teaches. It teaches what you appreciate and how the student's behavior, attitude, or response impacts others.

Be cautious of overpraising. It can be counterproductive. Heaping lavish praise on natural development can send a message to the student that your expectations for her were really not all that high.

If your Teacher Talk is, "Wow. That's unbelievable," when a student writes a decent paragraph or scores well on an exam, you communicate that you didn't expect her to do that well. Your words work against your desire to develop self-confidence and internal motivation.

Instead of saying, "That's unbelievable," use descriptive praise to communicate what you see. Tell her, "This is the highest score you've created this semester," or "These three examples helped me understand the point you were making." Describing her results insures that you don't send the message that you were surprised by her accomplishment.

THE VOICE OF DEBRIEFING

What if there were a simple way to encourage students to think critically and stay conscious of the choices they are making as well as the effect those choices have on themselves and others? What if that strategy also allowed students to become proficient at self-examination and self-evaluation? What if that same classroom technique helped students see mistakes as opportunities for growth, pointed them in the direction of learning, and did not make them wrong in the process? That would be exciting, wouldn't it?

What if that method could be used with young students as well as teenagers? What if it cost nothing and you didn't have to wait for it to come in the mail? What if you could start using it today with your students in your classroom? That would be positive and helpful, right?

Guess what? There is a strategy that does all of that and more. It's a verbal skill that we choose to call *debriefing*. Sadly, this amazing technique, the voice of debriefing, is not often used in educational settings today. It is a missing link in the process of delivering an effective education to students.

Why is it missing? And what does it link? Read on and determine for yourself if this voice has been missing in your Teacher Talk. Determine where and when you would be willing to put it to use. See if you want to use this technique to help your students take a look at their behaviors and learn from them.

"I'll be collecting your assignments now."

Vera was a high school senior who was horse crazy. She loved horses and did whatever she could to be near them in her spare time. She owned a horse and spent hours at the boarding stable: brushing, combing, cleaning, exercising, riding, and loving her horse in as many ways as she could invent. So when one of her high school teachers gave a service assignment that was required for graduation, Vera knew just what to do. The assignment, one that all students needed to complete to be eligible to graduate, involved doing charity work: giving of your time and energy doing service for another.

Vera went to another boarder at the stable and inquired if she could clean his horse's stall for a month. No compensation needed or desired. She explained the school assignment, telling the horse owner that she was required to do a month of loving service, write a three-page paper about the experience, and turn it in to meet the necessary service requirement for graduation. Upon hearing the explanation, the boarder willingly agreed.

When the free stall-cleaning time was up, the boarder asked Vera about the results of the assignment. "I turned it in," she said. "I got it back with a check mark on it indicating I had completed that requirement."

"What does the check mark mean?" asked the interested horseman.

"It means I got it done."

"No comments on it?"

"No."

"What did the other kids do for their assignments?"

"Don't know."

"Why?"

"They didn't share them."

"Did you talk about them in class?"

"Nope."

"You just turned it in, got it back, and that was it?"

"Yep."

Vera's teacher asked students to go out into the community and perform an act of service. Right on. He had them think about the experience and put those thoughts on paper. Right on again. So far so good.

Yes, a nice start, and this teacher stopped short of making this an extraordinary learning experience. In doing so, he missed an incredible teaching moment. Like a lot of adults, he failed to use the missing link. He neglected to activate the voice of debriefing.

> **"Get with your interaction trio. We're going to debrief this experience."**

"Read your papers to each other," a different teacher might have suggested. "When you are done, discuss how your experiences were the same and how they were different. We will all share some of those in a moment."

This teacher asked students to compare and contrast (a higher-level thinking skill) how their papers were and were not similar. He gave them a real reason to listen to each other's experience and something specific to look for.

When the trios finished, the teacher heard a report from each group. He then asked the class to make a list of what they could induce (inductive thinking) from their experiences. What generalizations could they make?

Had Vera's teacher invested the time to debrief the service assignment, his students might have offered:

"It felt good to do it."

"Other people like it."

"It's scary at first, but you get over it fast."

"I like myself for having done that."

"There are a lot of ways you can contribute to the community."

"Little things can make a big difference."

Yes, little things can make a big difference. A little thing like debriefing can lead to a wide variety of thinking and learning experiences. It can help solidify the learnings by making them conscious. It can promote increased feelings of self-esteem, the realization that giving and receiving are indeed one, and the important relationship between effort and accomplishment. It could have made a big difference, but it didn't, because in Vera's classroom the debriefing voice is not present. It remains a missing link.

> **"Let's talk about what happened at the assembly."**

The assembly consisted of a puppet show put on by a group of mothers who were working to eliminate bullying in the school. It was their first attempt at such a program, and the project did not unfold free from technical difficulties.

Student reaction to the bullying presentation was not respectful. Students laughed at inappropriate times, engaged in side conversations, and demonstrated a lack of interest in the topic and the presenters. Upon conclusion of the assembly, one fourth-grade teacher decided it was time to use her debriefing voice.

Marcy Mitchell knew that by debriefing she would be giving her students an opportunity to take a look at their behaviors and learn from them. This seemed to her like an ideal time to do just that.

The process of debriefing is pretty simple. Once students have had an experience, you invite them to reflect on it by thinking about it, writing about it, and talking about it. That is exactly what Marcy did.

Students had already had the experience: an assembly that had involved some malfunctions and inappropriate student reactions. "I want you to think about what just happened in the all-purpose room," she began. "Think about what you saw and what you heard. See if you can recall any of your thoughts or feelings that occurred when it was happening."

After waiting sixty seconds, Marcy asked students to take out their Responsibility Notebooks. "Find a clean page," she instructed. "Now, I want you to react in writing to a few comments I put on the board." Then she wrote:

1. On a scale of 0-10, mark the level of respect *you* showed during the assembly. Give a reason why you gave *yourself* the number you did.
2. On a scale of 0-10, mark the level of respect *our class* showed during the assembly. Give a reason why you gave *the class* the number you did.
3. What are three things we could do next time to show more respect?

After several minutes of writing, Marcy called, "Time."

> "Let me hear some of your reactions."

One by one, students who chose to share offered their interpretations and evaluations of the level of respect shown. Others chose to remain silent. There were some differences of opinion reported. All opinions were heard without judgment. Those who chose not to speak up publicly participated privately by silently comparing what they had written to the oral remarks of others.

"Let's make a list."

"Let's make a list of all the things we could do to show more respect next time," Marcy suggested. The list contained thirteen suggestions. The exact ideas this class produced are not important here. What is of importance is the process that led to the creation of that list and what happened next.

"Record this list in your Responsibility Notebook," Marcy instructed. "Now, put a star by the two items that you want to remember to do next time. These are the ones you see as the behaviors you can improve on. When we have another assembly, we will review these to remind ourselves of the goals we created."

This teacher helped her students create a vision of appropriate behaviors. Her debriefing focused on ways to improve. By having them record the specific behaviors to use next time, she helped them take one more step in the direction of attaining their goals.

"**Notice how you react if that pounding starts again!**"

The first step in effective debriefing is for students to have an experience or for you to create one for them. If there was a fight on the playground, students just had an experience. If eight students are late for your fourth-period class, they just had an experience. If Willie received a detention, he just had an experience.

In the situation involving the assembly, the experience presented itself with no warning. The teacher did not have to create it. It just happened.

Effective debriefing could follow the discovery of a note left by the guest teacher, an incident on the school bus, or student reactions to distractions created by renovations.

A middle school teacher noticed that his students were being distracted by drilling, pounding, and buzzing noises on the other side of a classroom wall. He knew what was going on. A sink was being built in the science room. Because of the commotion, many students were being distracted. That's when their teacher brought everyone's attention to it using these words: "Notice how you react if that pounding starts again. Pay attention to whether or not you notice it and how you respond. We'll talk about it in a minute."

This teacher waited until the pounding began again. He gave his students five minutes to react to it and then asked, "How many of you heard the pounding?" Several hands went into the air. "How did you react to it?" was the teacher's next question. Students' answers revealed a large level of distraction. This teacher walked slowly over to the board and wrote these words: HOW TO IGNORE A DISTRACTION.

> # How to Ignore a Distraction.

Using his teaching voice and the direct teaching method as outlined in the previous chapter, this educator wrote and explained the five specific things to do to ignore a distraction.

1. **Recognize the distraction**.

   "When you see yourself getting distracted," he told his students, "tell yourself that you're being distracted. If you aren't conscious that you're being distracted you have no power. Staying conscious gives you power. Now you are at choice."

2. **Give the distraction a name**.

   "If you can name it, you can tame it," he counseled his students. "Naming it takes the scariness away. Because it has a name, *distraction*, it's more easily handled."

3. **Make a decision not to be distracted**.

   "Set a positive intention for yourself," he told his students. "Once you have made a firm decision on the inside, outside forces will have less power over you."

4. **Refocus on what you were doing**.

   "Rereading the last paragraph, looking over the previous problem, or turning away from the distraction are ways to do this," he suggested. He offered other possibilities. They could cover their ears or move further away from the source of the distraction.

5. **Begin again**.

"Simply begin again," he explained. "Start anywhere, but begin somewhere. Repeat the entire process if needed. And always begin again."

After teaching his students how to ignore distractions, the teacher waited patiently for the noise to return. He didn't have to wait long. When it returned, he watched as his students practiced or ignored the skills he had just taught them.

> **"What evidence did you see that your classmates were ignoring distractions?"**

After watching his students deal with the noise level for a few moments, this professional educator placed two questions on the board.

1. What evidence did you see that your classmates were ignoring distractions?
2. What did your individual experience of ignoring distractions have in common with others?

Students were invited to respond to both questions, first by writing an answer and later by sharing with a partner. A group discussion followed and lasted seven minutes.

Asking these questions is a purposeful strategy designed to make the students' behaviors conscious to them. It asks students to look specifically at how they personally behaved and how others behaved. This requires thinking.

Indeed, the voice of debriefing can be used to stimulate a wide variety of thinking skills.

> **"What did you do that was respectful?"**

Questions that ask students to observe their own behavior and that of others and tell how or why they occurred require analytical thinking.

"Rate your effort to focus on the task on a scale of 0-10 and tell why you gave yourself that number."

"What evidence did you see that respect for the microscopes was happening?"

"What happened in your group that helped people stay on task?"

"Would you say we/you are getting better, staying the same, or getting worse with the task of sharing materials? Why?"

> ## "What do you think would have happened if . . . ?"

Questions that require thinking that reaches into the future call for making a prediction.

"Predict what would happen if we didn't follow the class creed."

"What is your guess as to the results if we do not get started quickly?"

"What is a possible result of forgetting to ask for makeup work?"

> ## "See if you can summarize in one sentence what you learned about owning your own behavior."

Summarizing requires a different kind of thinking, a kind that is often required on state assessment tests.

"If you could put all we have learned about organizing your science notebook in one phrase, what would it be?"

"What conclusion can you make for becoming skilled at criticizing the idea rather than the person?"

> ## "Which one was the best, in your opinion? The worst?"

Asking for thinking that requires evaluation or self-evaluation is yet another higher-level thinking skill that can be used with your debriefing voice.

"Rank order them from most to least helpful. Tell why you put the first one on top."

"What grade would you give our class on respect for the guest speaker? Explain your answer."

Many students have been trained to believe it is their job to do the work and an adult's job to evaluate it. Debriefing with questions that require student self-assessment, self-evaluation and self-appraisal teaches them self-reliance and helps them develop an inner authority.

> ## "How is the skill we learned today similar to the one we learned yesterday?"

When you ask, "How are they the same/different?," you are asking students to use another important thinking skill: comparing and contrasting.

"How is respecting the microscope the same as respecting the guest teacher?"

"List the differences in checking for your understanding and checking for your partner's understanding."

"In what ways are saying nice things and being kind to others the same and/or different?"

"What did your individual experience of talking responsibly have in common with what others reported?"

> ## "What could you do to improve your score on this?"

The necessity to help students create plans for improvement is another reason why the effective use of the debriefing voice is essential for teachers today.

"Wherever you placed yourself on the 0-10 scale, what would you do next time to move up two or more points?"

"What would our class have to do to create an A on this skill?"

"List two things you can do next time to improve on making an effective transition."

"What pattern do you see about your own behavior in regard to respecting others?"

Inductive thinking occurs when you ask students to make a generalization. It requires that they induce a conclusion or outcome based on several experiences.

"On the whole, what can you say about people who share their materials with others?"

"Generalize what can be expected of people who respect each other."

"Where else could you use this skill in your life?"

Application occurs when you take a skill you learned over here and put it to use over there. Are you able to apply it in other areas of your life?

If you teach a high school basketball player to respect his uniform, will he respect his business suit when he gets older? If you teach a child to use appropriate language in school, will she use it on the bus? If you teach a student to be kind and courteous in the art room, will he do it in the gymnasium? Maybe and maybe not.

You can increase your chances of having students integrate skills into their lives if you debrief regularly.

Reverend Bill came to us a few years ago with a problem. He was struggling with student behaviors he didn't feel were appropriate in his Christian high school. "I have wonderful teachers here," he told us. "They love the students and do a great job teaching. In our religion classes we teach about God's love, about caring, treating others the way you want to be treated, making amends, giving loving service, cooperating with others, and being nonjudgmental. And the students learn the material."

He went on to explain how students get good grades and pass all the tests in their religion classes. Most students can write well-constructed answers to complicated essay questions. Many are on the honor roll. A significant percentage of graduates go on to college.

Not hearing any cause for alarm, we asked Reverend Bill what the problem was. "They write down all the correct answers on the tests," he said, "and then they go out in the halls and rip each other's faces off. They put each other down and make fun of one another. They mock, ridicule, gossip, bully, and boast. It's not pretty. They know the spiritual behaviors and attitudes we teach. They just don't practice them in their lives."

Our recommendation was to increase the amount of debriefing that occurs in his classes. If you want a behavior, you have to teach a behavior. If you want more of that behavior, you have to structure it so students practice that behavior. And if you want to blow the incidence of the behavior off the charts, you need to debrief it consistently.

Debriefing is the piece that holds the entire process together. It's the piece that gives you the big jump in the application of the behavior, the using of it in other places in your students' lives.

> **"Turn to your partner and give each other a high-five."**

Another important use of debriefing is for celebrating success. Teachers often see the value of debriefing when things go poorly. Less often do they use it when things go well.

Yes, debrief if you find a negative note from the guest teacher on your desk the morning following your absence. Also debrief if that note is complimentary. Use it as an opportunity to celebrate.

Debrief if things went well on the bus during the trip to the aquarium. Debrief if the microscopes were returned properly to the shelf without a mishap. Debrief if the note the custodian left made a positive comment about the cleanliness of your classroom. Debrief if you walked through the lunchroom and noticed that students cleaned up after themselves immaculately.

"Record in your Responsibility Notebook two things you did that helped keep your lunch table clean for the next group."

"Put a big 'RIGHT ON' message on your recent goal that helped you get started quickly."

"What can you pat yourself on the back for in regard to staying focused today?"

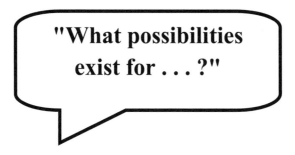

"What possibilities
exist for . . . ?"

Use your debriefing voice to produce possibility thinking in your students.

"What possibilities exist for improving this situation?"
"What ideas do you have for including others?"
"List some options we have for making amends."

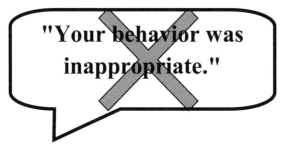

"Your behavior was
inappropriate."

"You left the lunchroom in an unacceptable state. I was embarrassed to walk through there. You need to focus more on cleanup. Pick up your straws, check for napkins and uneaten food. I know you can do better than that. Let's all try harder tomorrow."

This is not debriefing. This is telling. This teacher is not asking kids to think. He is doing their thinking for them. He is unaware that it is easier to dismiss information that comes from the outside than information generated on the inside.

> ## "Hiam, let's talk about your plan."

Up to this point, our examples of debriefing have focused on lessons with the entire class. Now we turn our attention to using this important voice, the debriefing voice, with individuals.

When Jean Paul returned from the Responsibility Room (the Responsibility Room will be covered in depth in the chapter on the voice of accountability) with his newly created behavioral plan, the implementation of that plan was left to him. After two days the Responsibility Room teacher called Jean Paul out of class. It was time to debrief.

"How's the plan working out?" was her first question. That began a debriefing discussion that lasted twenty minutes. Other debriefing questions posed to Jean Paul during that conversation included:

"What surprised you about the reactions you received?"

"Were you satisfied with your efforts to make amends?"

"What did you see happen as a result of implementing your plan?"

"What conclusions can you draw about this situation?"

"Do you have any ideas for tweaking your plan to make it better?"

"What part of your plan or effort to implement it deserves a pat on the back?"

Jean Paul did not write his answers. They were verbalized. When the discussion ended, Jean Paul went back to class. Before he returned, the Responsibility Room teacher set another date to talk (debrief) again. They would be meeting the following week to once again discuss, refine, and celebrate Jean Paul's efforts toward becoming more self-responsible.

> ## "How is Jean Paul's plan working from your point of view?"

Before the Responsibility Room teacher met again with Jean Paul, she met with his classroom teacher. Together they would debrief his classroom behavior and efforts to implement his plan.

"How is Jean Paul's plan working from your point of view?" was the first question asked to his classroom teacher. "What do I need to know so when I meet with him again I can help him be more successful with that plan?" followed. Once again twenty minutes were invested. Twenty minutes that were designed to keep this student heading in a healthy, uplifting, positive direction. Twenty minutes that would make the classroom teacher's instructional responsibilities easier to fulfill. Twenty minutes that would create a win/win for both the teacher and the student.

> # "I've been hearing some nice things about you."

"I met with your teacher," the Responsibility Room teacher confessed as she sat down with Jean Paul exactly one week later, as promised. "Mrs. Courtemanche had some nice things to say about you. Do you want to hear them?" And so another debriefing session began for Jean Paul.

A lot of time is being spent on one student, you might be thinking. "Spent" would be your word. Ours would be "invested." Is this student not worth this investment of time? Does he not deserve to be taught how to implement a plan and follow through with it? Does he not deserve to be given skills that can help him choose responsibility, respect, and self-control?

There is much to be learned through the use of these debriefing sessions. This student is learning to stay conscious, to make a plan for improvement, to evaluate the success of that plan, to shore up the weak spots, to analyze, predict, compare, rate, and celebrate his successes. Are these lessons not important because they are not measured on the test? Are they not of value because they cannot be quantified by the instruments you created to define an effective school?

We don't care how high your test scores are. If you leave this child behind, you do not have anything close to resembling an effective school!

"Let's look at some of
the decisions you made."

After the football team left the film room following their full-squad debriefing of Friday night's victory, the coach asked two players to remain. Yes, coaches debrief regularly. It's called time-out, half time, and video review. Because of those debriefing opportunities, changes can be made, improvement can be accelerated, and successes can be appreciated.

The two remaining players were quarterbacks, the ones entrusted with running the offense. "Let's look more closely at some of the decisions you made," the head coach began. Coach Karzan then invested another hour with his quarterbacks: looking at video, showing the defenses, talking about possible choices, examining results.

Did Coach Karzan do some direct teaching? Yes. Did he give these young players information they didn't have? Yes. Did he ask debriefing questions, allow the young athletes to have input and draw conclusions, and engage them in self-evaluation? Yes.

> ## "Time for another 3-D lesson."

Students in Ana Contreras's second-grade classroom were not surprised by these words. They had heard them many times before. They knew what to expect and it wasn't getting out their special glasses to watch a video in three dimensions. Rather, their teacher was about to do some teaching, followed by practice and then discussion. The three D's, as these youngsters knew full well, are Direct, Do, and Debrief.

For the first D, Direct, Ana uses both the T-chart and the direct teaching strategy to teach her students skills involved in interacting with others, assuming responsibility, and building character. Recently, she taught them what *asking for help* sounds and looks like. The resulting T-chart listed these items.

<u>Asking for Help</u>

Looks Like	Sounds Like
Raising you hand	"I would like some help with this, please."
Standing by the teacher's desk	"I don't understand. Will you show me again?"
	"Will you see if I did this right?"
	"I'm stuck. What do I do next?"

On another occasion, Ana used direct teaching to help students learn how to *clean up* after a cut-and-paste activity. The items on this list were:

<u>Clean Up</u>
1. Put magazines in scrap box.
2. Put lids on paste jars and return to shelf.
3. Throw scraps in basket.
4. Sponge off desk with warm water.
5. Wring out and return sponge to the sponge bin.

Whether the teacher uses a T-chart or direct teaching to communicate a skill set, the first D, Direct, is always followed by the second D, Do. This is where students get to "do" what is expected. They get to have an experience of doing what has been taught.

The third D is the essence of this chapter, Debriefing. Once again, this is the piece that encourages application, that gets students putting these skills to use in their own lives. Debriefing is the glue that holds it all together. Sadly, it is also the missing link in many families and classrooms around the world.

So what do you do if you use the 3-D method to teach appropriate skills and employ the missing link of debriefing on a regular basis and students still exhibit inappropriate behavior? What now?

It is now time to use another voice, the one explained in depth in the next chapter, The Voice of Accountability.

THE VOICE OF ACCOUNTABILITY

Let's assume you have learned to use the first four voices regularly and effectively: the voice of structure to create clear boundaries, routines, and rituals which produce a classroom structure that is clear and understood by all; the voice of nurture to communicate empathy, concern, and respect that builds positive relationships with your students; the voice of teaching to help students learn important interpersonal and responsibility skills. You have used that voice to instruct them in how to organize their history notebook, show respect for the guest speaker, budget time, get started quickly, ignore distractions, and implement other important life skills. Your voice of debriefing helps students examine their behaviors and learn from them. Your verbal skills give students opportunities to think critically, self-evaluate, learn from their mistakes, and set goals.

In spite of your efforts to skillfully use these various voices, some students still choose not to follow the class norms, ignore distractions, treat the microscopes respectfully, or complete their assignments on time. What now? Now is the time to turn to your verbal skill toolbox and implement another voice: the voice of accountability.

The accountability voice allows students to come face-to-face with personal responsibility by experiencing related, reasonable, and respectful consequences that flow naturally from their choices and actions. This voice is used to help students see themselves as cause of the outcomes they generate. Delivered with an open heart, the accountability voice allows students to experience the positive or negative consequences of their behaviors.

Implemented consistently, with gentleness and love, consequences can become the cornerstone of your discipline structure and your students' path to developing personal responsibility.

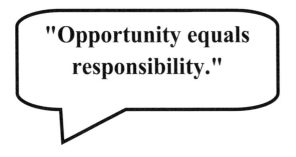

"Opportunity equals responsibility."

Kristy Hollister is an elementary school reading specialist in a small town in Pennsylvania. Recently, she constructed bookmarks for all her second- through fourth-grade reading club members. The message she selected for the bookmarks was an equation that reads: *Opportunity equals responsibility.*

When Kristy presented the bookmarks to her students, she explained to them how equations work. She informed them that when an equals sign appears in the middle of an equation, whatever is on either side of that symbol has the same value. She also explained that since the value is the same on each side, then what comes before the equals sign (6+2) is the same value as what comes after the equals sign (8). She also explained that any equation can be written in reverse order. If 6+2=8, then 8=6+2 is also true.

Kristy then applied the math logic to her bookmark equation. "Since *opportunity equals responsibility,*" she told her students, "then it is also true that *responsibility equals opportunity.*" To help her students grasp this mathematical concept and apply it directly to her situation, Kristy gave them the following two examples:

First, she told students they had the OPPORTUNITY to take a book from her room whenever they liked. Their RESPONSIBILITY was to return the book as soon as they were finished with it. If they followed through with the RESPONSIBILITY to bring the book back, they earned the OPPORTUNITY to take out another book. If they chose to neglect the RESPONSIBILITY of bringing their book back, then they chose not to participate in the OPPORTUNITY to select a new book on the next trip to her room. Instead, they got to look through books and magazines that must remain in the room while other students were selecting a book to borrow.

> **"In this room you have an opportunity to sit by a friend. Your responsibility is to stay on task and refrain from engaging in side conversations."**

For a second experience with the *opportunity equals responsibility* equation, Kristy told the students they had an OPPORTUNITY to sit next to a friend. Their RESPONSIBILITY was to stay on task and refrain from engaging in side conversations. If students chose to implement their RESPONSIBILITY, then the OPPORTUNITY remained the same. If their RESPONSIBILITY dropped, so did the OPPORTUNITY to sit by the person of their choice.

"I could tell there was a different feeling in the air when I implemented those two scenarios," Kristy said. "I didn't feel like I had to lecture them or enforce punishments. By simply giving them the consequence (positive or negative) they asked for, I think both the students and I felt like I was showing them increased respect."

The bookmarks, which stayed in the books, served as a visible and silent reminder that responsibility equals opportunity in the reading club room. Kristy noticed she was able to cut down on the number of times she had to remind students to bring their books back. She effectively shifted that responsibility from her back to theirs through the use of the bookmarks. By staying calm and consistent as she implemented the consequences, Kristy experienced less stress and gained increased cooperation from students who were now seeing themselves as responsible for the opportunities they were earning.

By connecting opportunities to responsibilities and putting students in charge of how they handled the equation, Kristy helped her students experience the relationship between cause and effect: when the responsibility is not accepted, the opportunity is temporarily lost. She also gave them abundant opportunities to demonstrate whether or not they were accepting the responsibility. Her efforts increased the chance that her students would learn that their choices affect the results that follow.

For more information on *Opportunity equals responsibility*, the Dynamic Discipline Equation, see our book, *The Only Three Discipline Strategies You Will Ever Need*, www.personalowerpress.com.

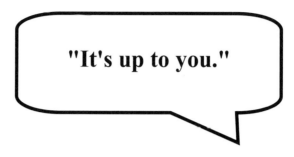

"It's up to you."

Estella Orgondo, a high school teacher in southern Florida, spoke to us recently at one of our frequent educator workshops. "Oh, I know what you mean with this discipline stuff," she told us. "I do this all the time. I did it just the other day with a student athlete. How about if I tell you what I did and what I said and you tell me if I did OK?"

We agreed, and she went on to explain, "Reggie is a wrestler and he had a big tournament coming up on the weekend. On Thursday I have to initial eligibility cards that the athletes present to me. If they're passing the class I sign it. If they're not passing I don't sign it. Every athlete must do this every Thursday with every teacher to be able to participate in sports that week. Reggie came to me on Monday and explained that he had a big tournament coming up that weekend and wanted to know if I was going to sign his eligibility slip on Thursday or not. He was behind in his work to the point where he was not passing my class. So I told him there were three assignments he had to complete. If he got them to me by Thursday, I would sign the card. If he didn't, I would not sign it. Then I told him, "It's your choice. It's up to you whether I sign it or not.'"

Estella then turned to us and asked, "How did I do?"

> ## Choose, Decide, Pick.

"It's clear to us that *you* understand the basic notion behind the concept that responsibility equals opportunity," we told her, "but we're not sure that *he* understands it. What we recommend is that you embellish what you told him by using the phrase, "responsibility equals opportunity," and frequently use the linking words *choose, decide,* and *pick.*"

"What do you mean?" she asked. So we gave her the following example of using the accountability voice.

"Reggie, as you know, in this classroom, responsibility equals opportunity. You have the opportunity to be on the wrestling team and compete in the events. As a student athlete, you also have the responsibility to keep your grades up. Right now, you are not passing this class. There are three assignments you have to complete to get up to a passing mark. If you choose to have them in to me by Thursday, you have decided to have me sign your card. If you pick the option to not have them in by that time, you have chosen to not have me sign it. In this classroom I let the student athletes decide whether or not they want to participate in sports. You know better than I do how badly you want to go to the tournament. So I let you choose the outcome. I look forward to seeing on Thursday what option you've picked."

If you were counting, you know that we used some form of the words *choose, decide* and *pick* seven times in a two-minute conversation. Do you think that's overkill? We don't. If you are talking to youngsters in that way today, you are a rare adult in their lives.

> **"If you choose to throw the blocks, you will be deciding to have a different activity this morning."**

Choose, decide, and *pick* are linking words that will help you add meaning and strength to the Dynamic Discipline Equation. They help students perceive the connection between cause and effect. They allow students to see that if they choose *this* they can create *that.* This style of Teacher Talk puts the student in control of the outcomes she creates in her life. It allows her to be decisive, empowered, and increasingly responsible.

Effective discipline calls for educators to structure consequences in a way that puts the student in control and allows him to feel responsible for the outcomes that result from his actions. Consequences are not used to control, manipulate, demonstrate power, or get even. Attempting to use consequences for control crosses the line and moves directly into the domain of punishment.

Punishment is force unrelated to the behavior and comes across as retribution. Disciplining from this stance places the child in a position of being "done to" by others in a position of authority. The child, feeling powerless, does not see himself as being in control of the outcome. He sees himself as the victim.

When students perceive that they are in control of whether or not they experience consequences or outcomes, they are empowered. They learn to see themselves as the cause of what happens to them. They realize that they personally create the results that show up in their lives by the choices they make. For discipline to be effective, it is necessary for children to feel they have power and control.

> **"If you choose to run in the hall, I will walk you to the bus for the next two days."**

When you use the important cause and effect linking words *choose, decide,* and *pick*, it is vital that you use them on both sides of your statement. Read and feel the difference in the examples that follow. In each paring, the first sentence has linking words on both sides of the statement. The second sentence has a linking word on only the first side of the statement.

Example 1

"If you <u>choose</u> to run in the hall, you are <u>deciding</u> to have me walk with you."

"If you <u>choose </u>to run in the hall, I will walk you out to the bus."

Example 2

"If you <u>decide</u> to use put-downs again, you are <u>choosing</u> to go to the Responsibility Room."

"If you_decide to use put-downs again, I'll be sending
you to the Responsibility Room."

Example 3

"If you choose to talk when I'm giving instructions,
you will be deciding not to sit by each other for a
while."

"If you choose to talk when I'm giving instructions, I
will move you away from each other."

Do you feel the difference? In the first sentence in each
example, who is the cause of the outcome? The student. In the
second sentence, who is the cause? The teacher. You can help
your students see themselves as cause and put them in control
of their own lives by using linking words on both sides of your
statement.

> **"If you decide to throw
> snowballs during recess, you are
> choosing to stand next to me."**

Communicating the Dynamic Discipline Equation
Opportunity equals responsibility effectively requires four
important steps.

**Step One: Explain the choices a student has and the
consequences that go with them *before* you implement any
consequence.**

"Jimmy, remember that at this school *opportunity equals
responsibility*. You have the opportunity to play with your
friends. You also have the responsibility to play in a safe way.

If you decide to throw snowballs during recess, you are choosing to stand over here next to me. You will be choosing to give up the opportunity to be over there with your friends."

This isn't intended as a threat or a warning. It is giving information and making sure the student is conscious of his choices. One big goal of using the accountability voice is to help students get and stay conscious of their behaviors and the choices they are making.

Step Two: Allow the student to choose the behavior and the consequence that accompanies it.

Do not tell the student which behavior to choose. If you do choose to tell him what to do, he will still choose whether or not to do it. Since he is the one making the final choice anyway, why not use your Teacher Talk to help him perceive himself as cause? At the same time, you are helping him become conscious of the choices available to him and the outcomes he could create.

Step Three: Respond immediately by implementing the consequence (positive or negative). Give no second chances.

If Jimmy chooses to throw another snowball, implement the consequence. Do not accept excuses. Do not give him one more chance. He doesn't get a try-over or a mulligan. He gets what he chose. Allow him to experience the consequence of having to stand by you instead of continuing to play with his friends during recess. You can use that time to debrief and give him information about safety and about the danger that throwing snow creates.

It is certain that the snow thrower will stand by the teacher if he chooses to throw snow. This consequence will happen every time. The student can depend on it. Knowing that, he can choose his next behavior with that in mind.

When a consequence occurs consistently, students can count on that fact and plan accordingly. They begin to see themselves as responsible for the outcomes they are creating in their own lives. Effective discipline that promotes responsibility calls for educators to use their accountability voice to structure consequences in a way that puts the student in control and allows him to feel responsible for the outcomes that result from his actions.

Step Four: Do give other opportunities to handle the responsibility later.

After Jimmy stands by you for a while, you can give him another opportunity to demonstrate he has learned about the danger of launching snowballs. At the very least, give him another opportunity during the next recess period.

All four steps need to be implemented with an open heart. Holding students accountable for their actions is a way of demonstrating that you care about them. Let the volume, tone, and words used in your accountability voice communicate that caring.

> **"I see you have chosen to have me sign [not sign] your eligibility card."**

Do follow through with consequences. Do give students what they chose. And do remember to use the words *choose, decide,* and *pick* when you do that.

A consequence need not be severe to be effective. It's not the severity of a consequence that has impact, it's the certainty. It is the certainty that specific, logical consequences follow specific actions that allows students to trust the discipline process.

What is certain in the case of the high school wrestler in Estella Orgando's class is that he will not be eligible for the tournament if he chooses to lower his responsibility by not turning in the appropriate work by Thursday. Yes, he will get another opportunity to become eligible the following week, and another opportunity to choose responsibility the week after that. This week he has chosen not to participate.

> ## "Just because I like you, do you think I should let you get away with it?"

Students often attempt to wiggle out of consequences. They come up with excuses, reasons, promises to be better next time, or thinly veiled threats.

One helpful way to react to those situations is by asking the student, "Just because I like you, do you think I should let you get away with it?" This question lets students know clearly that you will be holding them accountable for their actions. At the same time, it tells them you like them. This helps to separate the deed from the doer. "Just because I like you, do you think I should let you get away with it?" really communicates, "I like you, *and* the behavior you chose has consequences."

Creating a culture of accountability in your classroom is one of the most caring things you can do for your students. Holding students accountable communicates, "I care about you so much that I'm willing to set limits and design consequences that evolve from the choices you make concerning those limits. In addition, I care enough about you to follow through with the consequences that your behavior calls for."

Please hold students accountable for their actions. Before you do, make sure those consequences are related, reasonable, and delivered respectfully.

> "Putting other people down gets you one more page of writing sentences, Arwa."

What does writing sentences have to do with putting people down? Nothing. For a consequence to be effective and not exposed immediately for the pure punishment that it is, it needs to be *related* to the choice the student made.

"If you continue to choose to put others down, Arwa, you will be choosing to spend some time, energy, and effort learning to talk to people in a new way. You will be choosing to create an improvement plan in the Responsibility Room."

Writing sentences is not related to putting people down. Making an improvement plan is.

If when you don't return library books on time you miss gym time, the consequence is not related. If when you don't return library books on time you lose the opportunity to check out new books, the consequence is related.

If when you open your cell phone during class you get sent to the principal's office, the consequence is not related. If when you open your cell phone during class the teacher holds it for you until the end of class, the consequence is related.

If a consequence is unrelated to the behavior, it is interpreted in the student's mind as punishment. The student's focus is then likely to be on the person applying the punishment rather than on his or her own choice of behavior. He is not thinking about what he could learn from his choice or what he could do differently next time. He is focused instead on the adult and what is being *done to* him.

> "That's it. Give me your cell phone. You can get it back next week."

Another consideration when designing consequences is to ask yourself, "Is it *reasonable?*"

Some educators search for a consequence that will be strongly felt, thinking that if it hurts enough the student will be sure to retain the lesson. We disagree. Again, it's not the severity of a consequence that has the impact, it's the certainty!

The certainty that specific related and reasonable consequences follow actions allows students to trust the structure. Over time, they come to experience the structure provided by consistent consequences as secure and are then able to relax into the clearly defined boundaries. Your consistency in implementing consequences is the glue that holds a culture of accountability together.

Keeping a cell phone or electronic game for a week is not reasonable. Holding it for third period is. Sitting in the back of the room with your back to the class is not reasonable. Having your seat moved away from a friend for a day is. Being marked down for a late paper is reasonable. Having your paper ripped up in front of the class is not.

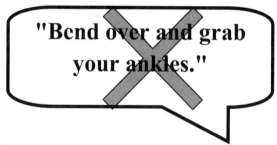

It is legal to use corporal punishment in twenty of the fifty states. There is a name for a big person who hits little ones. That name is BULLY.

If your students perceive you as a bully, you have lost stature in their eyes. When a spanking occurs, the student disconnects. He withdraws emotionally from you and the situation. With enough spankings the disconnect can become permanent. You have now damaged the relationship and injured your reputation in the heart and mind of your own student.

Spanking a student meets the needs of the adult, not of the student. By satisfying your needs, you can quickly return to your own agenda. Sacrificed in the process is the classroom agenda, including the opportunity to debrief, listen, seek consensus, and model that process for impressionable young people. If a healthy relationship with students is important to you, you undermine that goal by relying on the selfishness of spanking.

Spanking takes you in the opposite direction from becoming the educator you always wanted to be. Do you really feel like an effective educator when you spank students? Does your image of yourself increase when you resort to hitting them? Do you say to yourself, "There, I've been a good educator again," when you lay your hand on a student's backside? If you have a grander vision of yourself as an educator than one who models "might makes right" to his students, then spanking won't get you there.

Justifying in your mind the notion that spanking school children is necessary allows you to stay unconscious about the work you need to do on your own anger and power issues. It stunts your growth as a mature adult and permits you to continue acting like a child who is attempting to educate students. Hitting students helps you stay little and does nothing to encourage you to move into mature adulthood.

By jumping to the physical punishment stance, you lose an opportunity to learn enlightened discipline skills. Not only does this strategy rarely teach the lesson you intend, it also deprives you of learning new verbal skills and teaching techniques that would add to your educational toolbox. If the only tool you have is a hammer, you tend to look at everything as if it were a nail. Your effectiveness as a professional educator is hurt by relying on physical punishment and not developing additional skills.

When you discipline a student with physical aggression, you often initiate a power struggle. This activates resistance, reluctance, and resentment in the one who has received the discipline. Even if the student acquiesces, she often engages in revenge fantasies. That means she is wishing she could get you. If your spankings result in reluctance and resistance on the part of your students, once again it is you who has been hurt by damaging their image of you and their trust in you to protect them and keep them safe.

Threatening a spanking does not build personal responsibility in young people. At best, it induces forced compliance. It creates blind obedience that is directed from the outside. It does little to build self-discipline or self-responsibility. The student's inner authority is bypassed and he learns to rely on outer control from someone bigger and louder. What happens when the outer control leaves? Who controls the child now? How does a child function without an inner set of controls, ones he has not yet learned to trust?

You are a teacher. Spanking teaches that violence is the way to solve problems. The lesson is learned by the one who receives it, the ones who observe it, and, yes, even the one who inflicts it. Is that want you want to teach?

Hitting students does not fall within our definition of a reasonable consequence. Neither do some other strategies we have observed.

"You just lost your recess."

"There goes your gym period."

"That's five minutes. Do you want me to subtract more?"

"Hey, go ahead, fool around. It's your gym period, not mine."

Using the consequence of keeping recess or gym from a student is tantamount to cutting your own throat. The student you're threatening is likely the student who most needs to get out and exercise, blow off steam, and take a break. Without that much-needed movement, he is now more likely to be disruptive, activate his attention deficit tendency, and have trouble concentrating on the task at hand when instruction resumes.

Learning occurs best in a body that is awake and alert. When you limit physical activities to coerce students to comply, you undermine learning. Beyond the fact that we have an obesity epidemic in this country, limiting gym and recess renders the student less receptive to learning.

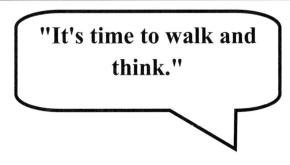

"It's time to walk and think."

"You're on the wall. Go sit by the wall until the bell rings."

"OK, you've just lost ten minutes."

"You obviously don't want recess today."

"There goes your recess."

Comments like these have been uttered by teachers as well as by recess and lunchroom monitors for decades. Withholding or threatening to withhold recess in an effort to induce a desired behavior has been going on for so long without a major shift in children's behavior that it makes us wonder who it is that's really the slow learner in this situation.

Good news. Teachers in an elementary school in Wyoming have come up with a viable and workable alternative to the denial of recess. They call it *walk and think.* Students in their school who choose inappropriate behaviors use recess time to walk (get exercise) and think (reflect and re-form). It works like this.

1. When a student chooses an inappropriate behavior such as put-downs in the classroom or shoving another child on the playground, they get one reminder. Notice we didn't say they get one warning. A warning is a threat. At this school teachers DO NOT threaten children! They remind them. That reminder is delivered in the form of the One-Minute Behavior Modifier explained in depth in our book,

The Only Three Discipline Strategies You Will Ever Need. It sounds like this: "Cara, that is a put-down. We don't put other children down in this class because people could feel bad and it often leads to physical violence. What we do here is tell the other person how we are feeling and what we would like to have happen. If you choose to put people down again, you have chosen to *walk and think* at recess."

2. If the child activates the behavior again, the adult in charge calmly says, "Cara, that is a put-down. We don't put other children down in this class because people could feel bad and it often leads to physical violence. When you choose to put others down, you choose to walk and think. You will need to draw a slip from the think tank to use at recess time."

3. The think tanks in this school vary in size and shape. One is actually a big plastic jug with an opening at the top large enough for a child's hand to enter. It contains several slips of paper with think topics on them. Here are some of the topics:

   - What effect does the behavior you chose have on the class? On yourself? Think both short-term and long-term.

   - How could you make amends for this behavior? Come up with three possibilities.

   - In what other ways could you get what you want other than the behavior you chose?

   - What did you learn from choosing this behavior? About yourself? About the others involved?

   - How could you remember to choose a different behavior next time?

- What do you intend to do next time? Why?
- Come up with an alternative behavior. Predict what would have happened if you had chosen that behavior.

4. During recess, the student takes a think strip from the think tank and holds onto it as she walks and thinks. Students are not allowed to use a pen or pencil to write their responses. This is not another in the long line of paper-and-pencil activities that students are subjected to frequently. The students are encouraged to think through their responses as they walk. Walking is done in a designated area, and the student is expected to keep moving for the duration of the time set. This is a time for thinking *and* for exercising.

5. When recess is over, a debriefing takes place. This can be done immediately if time and the structure of the day permits. Or it can be handled at a later time when the teacher is free to debrief effectively. Debriefing, which takes from three to six minutes, allows students to explain their thinking, what they learned, and their goals for next time. The emphasis here is on helping students learn lessons in self-responsibility and on creating plans for improvement.

Students add their goals and learning to their Responsibility Notebooks at this time. This adds a written component to the activity and creates a permanent record that can be reviewed later.

Walk and think is a major effort on the part of a concerned professional staff to turn a punitive, threatening activity into one that helps students develop self-responsibility, self-motivation, and self-discipline without losing recess and exercise time. It is designed to help students develop their inner authority, which is the only authority they take with them everywhere they go.

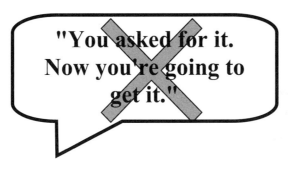

In addition to being related and reasonable, consequences need to be delivered in a respectful manner. To implement a consequence respectfully, begin with a tone that reflects serious concern but not a catastrophe. Think of your face as a second voice. You want your face to communicate the seriousness with which you treat this situation but not indicate this is the end of the world.

To do this, you have to set your angry feelings aside. If your accountability voice is full of anger, students look directly at you. Do you want them to tune into your anger, the veins popping out of your neck and your contorted facial expressions, or to the verbal message you're attempting to deliver? Do you want them to look outside themselves or inside themselves? You increase the odds of your message being heard if you speak calmly, firmly, and seriously.

This isn't always easy to do. After all, you're angry. Therefore, you might consider doing what David Helter did when he returned from one of our seminars to find a note on his desk left by the guest teacher. He moved up before he moved in.

Move Up Before You Move In

The morning of his return to school, David found the following message from the guest teacher:

"I had a very frustrating day. I found your class of sixth-graders to be immature and disrespectful. I had trouble quieting them down, their listening skills seemed nonexistent, and they frequently put each other down. I gave two students detention notices. Brandon Haller and Justin Semanski refused to cooperate. I finally sent them to the office. Although they were the biggest troublemakers, several other students contributed to the overall negative atmosphere. Some students were cooperative and respectful, but not many. You sure have your hands full here. Good luck the rest of the year."

David read the note three times. He had no trouble visualizing the picture painted by the guest teacher. Each time he read it, his anger climbed to a new level.

Possible consequences rushed through his mind. Fragments of lecture bursts formed as he mulled over how to respond to the situation created by his eleven- and twelve-year-old students. As he waited for them to arrive for class that morning, David prepared himself to move in with the words and actions he felt his students deserved. It was at this point that he recalled something he had learned the day before at our seminar: *Move up before you move in.*

Although the move-up-before-you-move-in concept had been new to him, David immediately recognized it as a strategy he could use. He knew it could help him be the type of teacher—the type of person—he really wanted to be. He'd had no idea he would be putting it to use so quickly.

What David learned at the seminar was this: before you move in to deal with a situation it's important to take time to move up—to a higher consciousness, to a higher self. He knew he would have to rise above this particular situation in order to avoid taking it personally. He realized he would have to raise his consciousness in order to free himself from the emotional snarl he had felt when he first read the note. He knew that if he didn't want to add the energy of frustration and anger to the volatile mix, he would have to detach emotionally from the situation. Not wanting to create a struggle, and desiring to say whatever he was going to say in a respectful way, he decided that the most effective way to stay off the battlefield was to rise above it. David decided to *move up* before he *moved in*. He took the last few minutes before his class arrived to put the skills he had learned the day before into practice.

> **Talk to yourself before you talk to the student.**

David reminded himself not to take the situation he found himself confronted with personally. "This is not about me," he told himself. "This is about my students— their behaviors, their beliefs, their choices. It is not a reflection on my teaching or who I am as a human being." He knew that if he could disconnect his ego from the events that had transpired he would be more likely to respond to his students' needs and motivations rather than to his own unconscious needs to influence their actions.

See it all as perfect.

Using another newly acquired skill, David decided to see the situation as perfect. "It's all perfect," he repeated to himself a few times. If his students had been respectful and cooperative, he reasoned, that would have been perfect—the perfect time to celebrate and congratulate them for their behavioral choices. Since they had chosen to be disrespectful and uncooperative, that was perfect, too. It was the perfect time to help them look at their behaviors and learn from them. David knew that if he told himself the situation was terrible, awful, and a pain to deal with, he would not be moving up in consciousness. But by realizing the situation was indeed perfect, he continued to ascend.

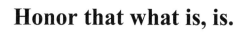

Honor that what is, is.

"What is, is," David thought to himself. He remembered that any time spent wishing, hoping, or "shoulding" (things should be different) was time that would not be invested in solving the problem. He knew he had to accept the "isness" of the situation emotionally before he could effectively search for solutions to improve it.

Make no assumptions.

Difficult as it was, David decided not to treat the note from the guest teacher as absolute truth. He wanted to hear another perspective, one from the students' point of view. From his newly created perspective of not taking the situation personally, realizing that it was perfect, refusing to resist it emotionally and making no assumptions, David quickly created a few ideas to present to his class. When the bell rang and his students began filing in, he was ready.

> ## "I have several questions to ask."

"Please take out a piece of paper," David directed his students after the morning routines were completed. "I have several questions I want to ask you concerning the events that transpired yesterday when the guest teacher was here. Please respond privately and nonverbally."

David used the whiteboard to create a continuum numbered from 1 to 10. "Rate yourself on this Respect the Guest Teacher Scale," he suggested. "Ten means you were respectful the entire day. Zero means you were totally disrespectful. Place an X where you feel you personally belong on the scale. Then write a two-sentence explanation that tells why you placed yourself where you did on the continuum.

"Now do the same thing on another continuum," he continued. "Only this time, think in terms of the entire class. How respectful was the class to the guest teacher? Once again, give me a two-sentence explanation.

"Next, complete the following three sentence starters."

The sentence starters David assigned were:

- I was being respectful when . . .
- I was being disrespectful when . . .
- One thing I could do to be more respectful next time is . . .

After using his debriefing voice to propose the questions, David sat back and watched as his sixth-graders struggled with the thinking skills he had set before them. The point of the assignment—self-appraisal, self-evaluation, and self-reflection—was to help his students become conscious of their behaviors on the previous day and give him information about their perceptions.

> "Let's make a list of what we learned."

When the students had finished writing their responses, David put them in groups to compare and contrast answers. He then heard a report from a spokesperson from each group. Following the reports, David asked students to generate a class list of what they had learned during the activity. This is the list they created.

- Some of us were more respectful than others.
- Most of us could have been more respectful.
- Some students use a substitute teacher as an excuse to act up.
- Substitute teachers overreact.
- One student's behavior can reflect on the entire class.
- We can do better.
- It's easier to behave when Mr. Helter is here.

With the list complete, David had each student begin a Respect and Responsibility Notebook. Their first entries included their personal responses to the self-appraisal debriefing questions and the class's list of what they had learned. He then had his sixth- graders add a paragraph detailing what they intended to do differently next time.

The debriefing now complete, David moved on to social studies. Before he did so, however, he paused a moment to give himself a mental pat on the back to acknowledge his efforts to put what he had learned at the seminar into practice. He liked what he had chosen to do, he liked who he had chosen to be, and he liked the results. He was grateful that he had learned to move up before he moved in.

Moving up before you move in can be used before you speak in any of the five voices. You can apply it before you use the voice of nurture to deliver an empathic response. If you move up before you speak, your empathy will be more likely to resonate with the student. Moving up before you structure, teach, or debrief also increases the likelihood that the words you use will be heard.

Moving up before you move in with the voice of accountability does not guarantee that students will make different choices next time, but it does guarantee that you are communicating in an increasingly respectful manner.

"It looks like a bunch of slobs ate in the lunchroom today."

A respectful voice of accountability refrains from using words that attack character or personality. Instead, they speak to the situation. "You're messy" speaks to the person. "There are papers and crayons on the floor" points to the situation.

"You're never going to learn" focuses on the person. "Looks like the paint brushes weren't rinsed out" draws attention to the paint brushes and the problem at hand.

Another way to increase the chance that your accountability voice is respectful is to remember to use the linking words of *choose, decide*, and *pick*.

"Sounds like you *chose* to have me write you up for the Responsibility Room."

"Since you *chose* to get this in on time, you've *decided* to have me sign your eligibility slip."

"Looks like you *decided* not to ride the bus for three days."

"Since you've *chosen* not to sit on the sofa quietly during story time, you've *decided* to sit on the circle. Please find another spot to sit."

Your goal is to allow the students, not you, to have control over whether or not they experience the consequence. Please respect both them and their choice as you allow them to experience the outcomes of that choice.

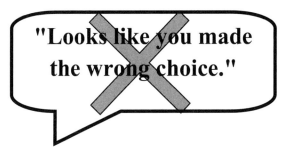

Making students wrong for their behavior is counterproductive to raising responsible young people. An effective voice of accountability does not make students right or wrong for their behavior. It simply holds them accountable for it without attaching an evaluation or making a judgment.

If a student fails to wear his white shirt and black slacks for the choir concert, don't make him wrong. Don't make him lazy. Don't make him forgetful. Don't make him irresponsible. Just make him someone who doesn't get to participate in the concert—the consequence you agreed on earlier.

Even if the problem reoccurs over time, refrain from making your students wrong. Blaming and faultfinding won't help them learn how to make different choices and behave differently in the future. Fixing the problem is more important than fixing blame. Join with your students in the search for solutions, and model for them that you value solving problems more than you do assigning blame, handing out punishments, or making them wrong.

> **"Looks like you don't get it yet. I'll have to increase the penalty."**

A student's compliance or noncompliance has nothing to do with the effectiveness of a discipline system. When discipline strategies demand compliance, as when the adult keeps increasing the severity of the punishment until the student complies, children learn that adults have power and they don't.

When we choose to use consequences, the aim isn't to make students comply. The goal is to present choices, allow them to choose, and give them room to learn from the results of that choice. When you use your accountability voice with the consequence system, students learn a lesson from either positive or negative outcomes. This is about teaching and learning. It is not about punishing until you get your way.

> **"No, I'm not going to get you in trouble, but you might."**

One of our friends, a retired teacher, frequently accepts substitute teaching opportunities near her home. In one school where she subs regularly the discipline policy consists of one warning, a second warning, and on the third offense, "You're out of here." "Out of here" consists of a trip to the ISS (In School Suspension) Room.

She recently related the following story.

In a ninth-grade class a young man chose an inappropriate behavior. She gave him a warning. Shortly after the warning, he repeated the behavior. She gave him a second warning. Upon receiving warning number two, he looked at her and said, "You're going to get me in trouble."

Her response to this student, who was clearly not taking responsibility for his actions and instead assuming the victim stance, was this: "No. I'm not going to get you in trouble, but you might. You chose that behavior the first time and I gave you a warning. You then chose to repeat the behavior and I gave you a second warning. If you choose the behavior for the third time, you will be deciding to have me write you up for ISS."

The student's reaction? "See? I knew you were going to get me in trouble!"

This student is not at the present time ready to own his behavior. He thinks, talks, believes, and acts like a victim. And like a lot of students in the world today, he is in desperate need of adults in his life who will talk to him exactly the way this guest teacher did. This student, and many more like him, deserves teachers who are verbally skilled at using the voice of accountability.

Repetition is the key. One adult talking to this student one time in this way will not create major changes in attitude or beliefs. This student might require many experiences with language that raises his awareness of the role he plays in the cause and effect connection before his behavior reflects an owning of personal responsibility. This would happen more quickly within a system where the entire staff works together to build shared cognitions, a similar language system, and a culture of accountability throughout the school.

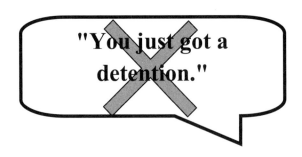

"That's a seventh hour for you, Mr. Jamison."

"You just earned a detention slip."

"It's In-School Suspension for you."

Take a close look at the language above. What do you notice about how we choose to describe the places where students are sent for breaking rules or demonstrating inappropriate behavior? We often describe these places using "detention," "suspension," or similar terms. These words and the Teacher Talk above suggest withholding, custody, retention, temporary removal, or a withdrawal of privileges. They have a decidedly punishment-oriented flavor to them.

We are professional educators with many years of training and experience. And the best names we can come up for these programs are *suspension* and *detention*? That tells more about us than in does about the students we assign to those programs.

Our choice of words is important. What we call these programs affects how we see them. How we describe them is critical to our mindset as we design and structure what occurs there.

> ## "I'm glad you're back from the Responsibility Room."

For instance, imagine that we called the area where students are sent following the use of inappropriate behavior the Responsibility Room. Would it alter how we see that place, as well as its function? Would it change what we choose to do with the students who demonstrate behaviors that land them there? We think it would.

In a Responsibility Room, students would come to learn lessons in responsibility. This is not unlike a student's going to the music room to learn music or to the science room to learn science. The name helps define its function. It helps us create the mindset we bring to the designing of what goes on there.

In a Responsibility Room, students would be expected to create a Responsibility Action Plan. That plan would include articulating the choices the student made that got her there in the first place. It would require a stating of the problem and a solution the student is willing to put into effect. Approval by both the student and the teacher would be necessary.

In the Responsibility Action Plan the student would identify and name the specific behavior that was inappropriate and set a goal for herself to alter it. She would articulate what she will do next time in place of the inappropriate behavior. This piece of the plan would be a stating of what she *will* do rather than articulating what she *will not* do. The goal would include specific behavioral indicators so everyone involved could tell whether the goal was being attained. Those indicators would describe what the behavior "looks like" and "sounds like." Each of those lists would include several examples.

Students developing a Responsibility Action Plan in the Responsibility Room would list the steps they intend to implement to achieve their goal. They would put in writing how they will know when they are making progress toward the goal.

Student, teacher, and parents would be required to sign the Responsibility Action Plan.

By changing the name of the In-School Suspension Room to the Responsibility Room, we change how we perceive it. When our perceptions change, so do our behaviors. Let's end detention and suspension rooms. Let's help students take a big step toward responsibility by taking the first step ourselves. It's time to create the Responsibility Room.

> **"Hello, Mrs. Radison. Richie chose some behaviors this morning that resulted in a Responsibility Room assignment from Mr. Tanner."**

Imagine a phone call to a parent in your school sounding like this: "Hello. Mrs. Radison? This is Miss Wilson, the assistant principal at the middle school. Richie chose some behaviors this morning that resulted in a Responsibility Room assignment from Mr. Tanner. That means he has a responsibility issue to work on for the rest of the day. He's working on ways to speak more respectfully to other students. He may be bringing a plan home for you to sign tonight. He's right here and he's going to tell you all about it. Here's Richie."

Using this system, the purpose of notifying parents would be to provide information about what is happening at school. It would not be a threat to the student or a punishment. It would be one of the natural outcomes of being assigned to the Responsibility Room. Its function would be listed in the accountability information that goes home to parents and students at the beginning of the year.

"Nice to have you back. I missed your smile. Tell me about your plan."

After a suspension, welcome the student back. Acknowledge his effort to plan and implement new behaviors.

"Welcome back. Looks like you got serious about this."

"Yes, this will help all of us create an emotionally safe environment. Thanks for putting the time in on it."

"Thanks for doing this. I have a feeling it's going to be a good day."

If the student follows through on the plan, affirm and celebrate his growth in responsibility. If the plan doesn't work for him, or if he doesn't work the plan, assign another Responsibility Room experience so he can redo it.

"So what surprised you about implementing the plan?"

Let's assume the student returned to your classroom after devising a plan in the Responsibility Room. Perhaps he executed it well, or maybe not. In either case it is time to activate your debriefing voice, detailed in a previous chapter.

"How do you feel your plan is going?"

"How did it work for you?"

"What needs to be tweaked?"

Debrief at the end of the day. Debrief two days later. Debrief a week after that. That's a lot of debriefing, you might think. Yes, it is. And again, debriefing is the glue that holds it all together. It's the piece that gives you the big leap into having your students really put these concepts to use in their lives. Don't let debriefing be the missing link in your classroom or in the lives of your students.

Why can't the Responsibility Room supervisor do the debriefing, you could be thinking. Let's dream here for a moment. What follows is our view of what it would take to run a Responsibility Room well. First, it would require two professional staff members—two educators who have both counseling backgrounds and experience with troubled youth. If you had two trained staff, one could remain in the classroom with students who are still there learning and working on respect and responsibility issues. The other would be freed up to visit classrooms, pulling students out of class one at a time, debriefing with them, celebrating successes, adjusting plans, giving encouragement. They could meet with the classroom teacher to find out his or her perspective on how the plan was working for the student. This person could follow up with parents and touch base with the student regularly.

This concept of two trained staff in the Responsibility Room is not going to happen in most schools. Schools do not have the money today to hire two people for this important room. Most schools where we live, in Michigan, are currently reducing staff. Schools simply do not have the necessary dollars today to properly fund a room where students can learn what is necessary to become productive learners.

Isn't it interesting that there aren't enough dollars available to help troubled students get what they need, yet we have enough money to spend millions of dollars on testing programs. Interesting priorities we have, eh? So the test scores are going up. So what? You just left some really important students behind.

> **"I'm wondering what you're going to do for restorative action."**

Restorative action is a behavior that makes amends for a disruptive or hurtful action that a student has previously chosen. It is part of a formal accountability process and is designed to foster the growth and development of the student. Again, this is not about punishment. It's a natural consequence that is designed to instruct and facilitate learning in the student.

The student is responsible for deciding how to make amends in joint consultation with the teacher, an administrator, or the Responsibility Room supervisor.

The student who showcased his middle finger during the taking of the class photo may choose to replace, with his own money or work, twenty-seven photos that have already been paid for. He may have to contact the camera person and schedule a new shooting, help him set up the risers, and lend a helping hand as he packs up when he's finished.

The student who makes ink marks on a desk could sand and varnish it to restore it to close to its original condition.

The student who puts others down may come up with a list of positive words and use them twenty times during the week.

Saying you're sorry is not enough. It is cheap forgiveness. It's too easy. It does not make amends. The relevant question is, how are you going to make up for the effect of your actions? The root word of *restorative* is *restore*. How will you restore the situation to its former condition?

> **"You asked for this punishment, so now you'll have to deal with it."**

The accountability voice never speaks of punishment. Punishment does not deter inappropriate behavior. Punishment leaves children feeling more hostile and more vengeful. It does not teach desirable behavior or even reduce the desire to misbehave.

What punishment does is encourage students to be more cautious next time so they don't get caught. No student in the midst of being punished says to himself, "I guess I'll have to be more honest and respectful next time." They are much more likely to say to themselves, "I'll have to be more sneaky, more careful in the future."

Consequences and punishment are not synonymous. We have heard teachers and parents who use those two words interchangeably. They say, "Here is your consequence," but they mean, "Here is your punishment." If you are using consequences with a punishment mind-set, know that it will not work.

Effective consequences are nonhostile and nonpunitive. A consequence is a natural and inevitable outcome of a specified behavior that is applied consistently and immediately. It is predictable because it is known ahead of time and understood by both the adult and the child.

It doesn't matter what you call the accountability strategy you're using. You can call it punishment, a consequence, or an outcome. It is not the action you take that determines whether it's a punishment or a consequence. It's HOW you take the action.

For example, a trip to the Responsibility Room could be a punishment if it is administered arbitrarily and capriciously without the student's having prior knowledge of the consequences of the action he or she took. If the Responsibility Room assignment is communicated with anger and disrespect, it is punishment. If it is being "done to" a student, it is punishment.

The same strategy could be a consequence if it is a natural outcome that is closely related to the behavior and is delivered consistently and respectfully. It is more likely to be a consequence if it is a logical extension of a student's choice and communicated with an open heart.

CONCLUSION

Only skill saves. If you're boating on a lake and your craft springs a huge leak and begins to sink, you'd better be able to swim. Knowing the theory behind how to swim or the history of swimming will not save you. Being able to recite a ton of research regarding swimming will not save you. Knowing memorable motivational quotes from famous swimmers will not save you. You either know how to swim or you don't. If you're skilled at swimming, you have a chance to make it to the shore. If you don't know how to swim, you're going under. If you don't have the skill that this situation, this moment, calls for, you are eventually going to sink.

The Teacher Talk Advantage is jam-packed with verbal skills that will help you negotiate the turbulent waters professional educators are expected to swim in today. What do you do when a student says, "I hate you," or "This sucks!"? How do you handle that? Research on teaching will not save you. Neither will theory or motivational quotes. You don't have time to look up an answer in your old college classroom management text. The answer won't be there anyway. You don't even have time to Google it. You have to respond NOW!

You either have the necessary verbal skills to respond effectively to those situations or you don't. You will sink or swim depending on the level of your verbal skills.

As you have seen, we've divided the verbal skills necessary for effective teaching into five areas: structure, nurture, teaching, debriefing, and accountability. While it makes some sense to use your structure voice before you debrief and your teaching voice before you hold a student accountable, there is no order or hierarchy to follow for each and every situation.

Imagine a scenario that involves your finding brushes still filled with paint left unrinsed in the sink. The voice of structure can be used to create boundaries and guidelines for the use of paint. On the other hand, you might choose the voice of debriefing to help students become conscious of the situation and make plans for improvement. Or you could do some direct teaching about paintbrushes using the voice of teaching. It doesn't matter which voice you decide to use in this moment. All are valuable.

So which voice should you use in that situation? It's your call. You are the professional in charge in your classroom. You know your students better than we do. None of the choices listed above would be inappropriate. You get to decide.

One voice we do not recommend you begin with in the scenario described above is the voice of accountability. Some educators and parents jump immediately to accountability when children choose inappropriate behaviors. In doing so they have skipped over important opportunities to teach and reteach. They have also missed a chance to design debriefing activities to help students become conscious. In most cases, we recommend you save the accountability voice until you have regularly used the other voices you have in your verbal skill set.

Our main job is to teach. When you use your voice of structure, you are teaching. You are teaching the importance of boundaries and healthy limits. You are teaching the reasons behind those limits.

When you use the voice of nurture, you are teaching. You teach that people are more important than things. You teach about the value of empathy and how to recognize and state feelings. You teach for emotional intelligence.

When you build a T-chart, you are teaching respect and responsibility skills. That voice, the voice of teaching, instructs about interpersonal skills, character issues, and other important life skills.

The voice of debriefing teaches. It teaches how to think critically, how to self-evaluate, and how to judge yourself against an internal standard. It teaches about setting goals, following through, and staying conscious.

The voice of accountability teaches. It teaches about the relationship between cause and effect. It teaches about self-responsibility. It teaches how and why making amends is important. It teaches that learning is more important than punishment.

You might be thinking that the things we advocate are not valued in schools right now. They aren't on the test. They're not a measure of an effective school. They're not part of what teachers are being asked to do.

We know that. Do it anyway. Just because the test makers don't see the value of these incredible lessons doesn't mean they're not important. Just because legislators who have never taught in a live classroom for even one day of their lives wrote a law doesn't mean that law serves your students effectively.

Do you really believe that the narrow way we define an effective school today is the definitive answer to what young people need to be successful in today's world? We doubt it.

Are we saying to disobey the law or refuse to do what your administrators are advocating? No. If you do, you will get fired. Work on upping the test scores. That isn't a bad thing. It just isn't the only thing. Think about this: If students learned to ignore distractions, get started quickly, and get back on task, would that not affect their learning? If they learned to take personal responsibility for their learning, would that work at cross-purposes with doing well on achievement tests? No. If they came back from the Responsibility Room with a plan that reduced their incidence of bothering classmates, would that not enhance the learning environment and impact the few items that are tested? Of course it would. You can use these voices while you work on the goals laid out by others. And simultaneously you can work on the goals that achieve what you know children need today. You can do both.

One final suggestion. Whatever skills, techniques, or strategies you use in your classroom, put them to the following four-question test.

1. Does it work?
2. Is it respectful?
3. Does it help you become the teacher you always wanted to be?
4. What does it teach?

Question One: Does it work?

Writing a kid's name on the board, threatening to call home, having him sit in the hall, sending him to the principal's office, giving him a detention; suspending her, withholding her star sticker at the end of the day, keeping her in for recess, making her copy sentences; yelling, shaming, counting 1,2,3, do not work. None of these options passes the four-question challenge.

Question Two: Are they respectful?

Are the five voices respectful? Do they pass the second question? Of course they're respectful. You couldn't have read this far without knowing that.

Question Three: Does the technique you chose help you become the teacher you always wanted to be?

That depends on who it is you want to be. Haven't you always wanted to be the teacher rather than the criticizer, shamer, or policeperson? Haven't you wanted the skills necessary to make yourself an inspirational educator who invites appropriate behavior while holding students accountable with an open heart regardless of the outcomes they choose? Haven't you always wanted to be an adult who makes yourself dispensable while allowing students to take increasing responsibility for their lives so they can become increasingly self-motivating, self-reliant, and self-responsible? Haven't you always wanted to be the center that holds, even as change, challenge, and sometimes chaos swirls around you? If so, you can use these five voices to be that teacher. And you can begin today.

Question Four: What does it teach?

The five essential voices we have described teach empathy, perception, critical thinking, respect, responsibility, integrity, cooperation, kindness, healthy limits, speaking up for yourself, self-responsibility, self-discipline, decision making, self-assessment, self-motivation, goal setting, personal power, solution seeking, record keeping, making amends, consensus seeking, owning your choices and behaviors, the connection between cause and effect, and other life skills.

If you work the skills, the skills will work for you. Yes, you have to practice, make mistakes, improve and do it differently next time. This verbal skills system as it grows through your increasing ability and use can transform your classroom. No, it won't happen overnight. It requires persistence. Practiced regularly and consistently over a period of time, these verbal skills will allow you to create a culture of respect, responsibility, and self-motivated learning.

No teacher gets perfect students. And no student gets a perfect teacher. What all students deserve to get is an educator who works at improving his or her professional practice—one who is willing to learn verbal skills that invite students to work on improving their attitude and level of responsibility and increasing their desire to learn and fulfill their potential. They deserve a teacher who is committed to learning, practicing, improving, and continuing to grow right along with his or her students. We invite you to be that teacher.

No student takes a year of third grade from you. No student takes a year of algebra from you. They all take a year of YOU for third grade, algebra, history, physical education, choir, Spanish, kindergarten, or whatever you happen to teach. You are the best thing you have to offer them. Give them a lot of YOU.

They're worth it. And so are YOU!

ABOUT THE AUTHORS

__Chick Moorman__

Chick Moorman is the director of the Institute for Personal Power, a consulting firm dedicated to providing high-quality professional development activities for educators and parents.

He is a former classroom teacher with over forty-seven years of experience in the field of education. His mission is to help people experience a greater sense of personal power in their lives so they can in turn empower others.

Chick conducts full-day workshops and seminars for school districts and parent groups. He also delivers keynote addresses for local, state, and national conferences.

He is available for the following topic areas:

FOR EDUCATORS

- Motivating the Unmotivated
- Achievement Motivation and Behavior Management Through Effective Teacher Talk
- Celebrate the Spirit Whisperers
- Teaching Respect and Responsibility
- Cooperative Learning

FOR PARENTS

- Parent Talk: Words That Empower, Words That Wound
- The Only Three Discipline Strategies You Will Ever Need
- The 10 Commitments: Parenting with Purpose
- Empowered Parenting

If you would like more information about these programs or would like to discuss a possible training or speaking date, please contact:

Chick Moorman
P.O. Box 547
Merrill, MI 48637
Telephone: 877-360-1477 (toll free)
Fax: 989-643-5156
E-mail: ipp57@aol.com
www.twitter.com/chickmoorman
www.facebook.com/chick.moorman
Websites: www.chickmoorman.com and
www.uncommon-parenting.com

Thomas B. Haller, MDiv, MSW, ACSW, DST

Thomas Haller is the chief parenting and relationship correspondent to WNEM TV 5 (CBS affiliate), MY5 TV, and WNEM News Radio 1250 AM. He has been the weekly radio personality for over five years on Mid-Michigan's number one radio station, WIOG 102.5 FM. Thomas is also the regular guest host of Health Line on WSGW 790 AM/100.5 FM. He has been a featured guest on over 150 radio shows, including such notable programs as Oprah Radio, Playboy Radio and The World Puja Network.

Thomas is a parenting and relationship specialist, the coauthor of five highly acclaimed books, a psychotherapist maintaining a 20-year private practice as a child, adolescent and couples therapist, a sex therapist, and a chronic pain counselor.

Thomas has a Master of Divinity degree, Master of Social Work degree and a Doctorate in Child and Family Studies. He has extensive training in psychotherapy with children and couples. He is a certified EEG biofeedback technician, an AASECT certified diplomate of sex therapy, and a certified sports counselor.

In addition, Thomas is the founder and director of the Healing Minds Institute, a center devoted to teaching others to focus and enhance the health of the mind, body, and spirit. He is president of

Personal Power Press, Inc., a small publishing house committed to providing parents and educators with practical material for raising responsible children. Lastly, Thomas and his wife, Valerie, maintain a not-for-profit 501 (c) (3) organization, Healing Acres, an equine retirement ranch enabling aged horses to live out their lives in a low-stress atmosphere.

He is available for workshops, seminars, student assemblies and commencement speeches.

Website: www.thomashaller.com
Twitter: www.twitter.com/tomhaller
LinkedIn: http://www.linkedin.com/pub/thomas-haller-m-div-lmsw-dst/1a/8/868
Facebook: www.facebook.com/thomas.b.haller
Blog: www.uncommon-parenting.com
E-mail: thomas@thomashaller.com

OTHER BOOKS AND PRODUCTS

www.personalpowerpress.com

<u>For Educators</u>

SPIRIT WHISPERERS: Teachers Who Nourish a Child's Spirit, by Chick Moorman ($24.95)

TEACHER TALK: What It Really Means, by Chick Moorman and Nancy Weber ($15.00)

TEACHING THE ATTRACTION PRINCIPLE TO CHILDREN: Practical Strategies for Parents and Teachers to Help Children Manifest a Better World, by Thomas Haller and Chick Moorman ($24.95)

MOTIVATING THE UNMOTIVATED: Practical Strategies for Teaching the Hard-to-Reach Student, audio seminar featuring Chick Moorman ($95.00)

<u>For Parents</u>

PARENT TALK ESSENTIALS: How to Talk to Kids about Divorce, Sex, Money, School and Being Responsible in Today's World, by Chick Moorman and Thomas Haller ($15.00)

PARENT TALK: How to Talk to Your Children in Language That Builds Self-Esteem and Encourages Responsibility, by Chick Moorman ($15.00)

THE ONLY THREE DISCIPLINE STRATEGIES YOU WILL EVER NEED: Essential Tools for Busy Parents, by Chick Moorman and Thomas Haller ($14.95)

TEACHING THE ATTRACTION PRINCIPLE TO CHILDREN: Practical Strategies for Parents and Teachers to Help Children Manifest a Better World, by Thomas Haller and Chick Moorman ($24.95)

THE 10 COMMITMENTS: Parenting with Purpose, by Chick Moorman and Thomas Haller ($19.95)

THE LANGUAGE OF RESPONSE-ABLE PARENTING, audiocassette series featuring Chick Moorman ($39.50)

PARENT TALK FOCUS CARDS, by Chick Moorman ($10.00)

THE PARENT TALK SYSTEM: The Language of Response-Able Parenting, Facilitator's Manual, by Chick Moorman, Sarah Knapp, Thomas Haller, and Judith Minton ($300.00)

DENTAL TALK: How to Manage Children's Behavior with Effective Verbal Skills, by Thomas Haller and Chick Moorman ($24.95)

For Couples

COUPLE TALK: How to Talk Your Way to a Great Relationship, by Chick Moorman and Thomas Haller ($24.95)

Qty.	Title	Price Each	Total
	Subtotal		
	Tax MI residents 6%		
	S/H (see chart below)		
	Total		

Please add the following shipping & handling charges:
$1 - $15.00 -- $4.95 $15.01 - $30.00 -- $5.95
$30.01 - $50.00 -- $6.95 $50.01 and up 15% of total order
Canada: 20% of total order. US funds only, please.

Ship To:
Name: _____
Address: _____
City: _____ State:_____ Zip: _____
Phone: _____
☐ **American Express** ☐ **Discover** ☐ **VISA**
☐ **MasterCard** ☐ **Check/Money Order**
(payable in US funds)

Card #_____-_____-_____-_____
Expiration Date _____/_____
Signature_____

PERSONAL POWER PRESS, INC.
P.O. Box 547, Merrill, MI 48637
Phone: (877) 360-1477 - Fax: (989) 643-5156 - E-mail:
customerservice@personalpowerpress.com
www.personalpowerpress.com

NEWSLETTERS

Chick Moorman and Thomas Haller publish FREE e-mail newsletters for parents and educators. To subscribe to either of them, e-mail:
customerservice@personalpowerpress.com

Or you can visit:
www.personalpowerpress.com.

BLOG

Uncommon Parenting Blog:
www.uncommon-parenting.com

The Teacher Talk Advantage Training Opportunities

Awareness Session

Features effective ways of talking to students that enhance self-esteem, stimulate learning, and encourage autonomy. Increases a teacher's ability to deal with typical daily situations and problems faced by all teachers while communicating and expecting respect. Includes the 10 best/10 worst things you can say to your students. Intended to give enough Teacher Talk information so educators can see the advantage in scheduling further training and skill development in this topic.

Full-Day Presentation

This six-hour presentation helps an entire staff develop shared cognitions, a mutual language, and Teacher Talk techniques that can be implemented uniformly throughout the school. It is designed to help staff become skilled at defusing and handling anger, using effective praise, communicating expectations, and holding students accountable without wounding their spirit. Verbal skills that greatly reduce inappropriate behaviors, encourage difficult-to-motivate students, and teach respect and responsibility are included. This one-day seminar equips staff with the skills necessary to return to the classroom with an important and positive advantage when working with their students.

Book Study Group

The Teacher Talk Advantage Book Study Kit

This study kit includes a hardback copy of *The Teacher Talk Advantage*. You will have access to t*he Teacher Talk Advantage* Book Study web site where you can download:

1. A copy of your workbook.
2. Audio recordings by authors Chick Moorman and Thomas Haller introducing each section of the book study, posing questions, suggesting discussion topics, and giving clarifying information.
3. 300 Teacher Talk Quick Tips.

In this book study kit you are invited to read, discuss, and make journal entries on the important concepts covered. If you are part of a book study group you will have regularly scheduled meetings and discuss many of the topics with your colleagues. If you are doing the study kit alone you can create a pace of study that works best for you. You can go as fast or as slow as you choose. Whether you are doing this alone or with a group, the end goal is successful implementation of the ideas and concepts being presented.

By ordering the Building Level Kit you obtain the right to copy all materials for your staff and the codes that enable your team to access the audio recordings.

Three-Day Staff Training

Includes more material than the one-day session, more skill practice, and debriefing of the previous session. This training can occur in three back-to-back days or be spread out throughout the year. Includes a price break for multiple days.

Observations and Coaching

The authors are available for observation and coaching at your school upon request. This could include individual and/or entire school coaching. Includes observations, written descriptive feedback, and face-to-face communication. Telephone coaching is also available for individuals upon request.

Training of Trainers

This three-day skill-based training helps local facilitators teach educators how to use verbal skills to create responsible, motivated, achieving students. It includes techniques to assist trainers in learning communication strategies that revolve around the Five Voices of Effective Teaching: Structure, Nurture, Teaching, Debriefing, and Accountability. Participants learn training strategies that allow them to teach the Teacher Talk Advantage with expertise and confidence. Ongoing technical assistance is provided to all graduates.

The facilitator training is designed to prepare local trainers to skillfully present the Teacher Talk Advantage to educators in their school district. Materials included with training are a facilitator's manual, PowerPoint slides, participant workbooks, DVD, evaluation forms, logos, and the hardcover Teacher Talk Advantage book.

Private Web Site Access

This web site is offered to participants who have completed at least one day of training in the Teacher Talk Advantage. It includes special articles, tips, audios, and discounts on Teacher Talk Advantage products.

Personal E-mail Access

Personal e-mail access is provided to give you faster and more direct access to the authors, get your questions answered more quickly, and create a personal and ongoing connection.

Retainer

For school staffs that want to make a serious commitment to learning and implementing the skills involved in the Teacher Talk Advantage. Guarantees you top priority in date selection and lowest daily rate offered. Must include ten days or more, which can be spread out over two school years.

Website

www.teachertalkadvantage.com

Contact Information

Chick Moorman
Telephone: 877-360-1477 (toll free)
Fax: 989-643-5156
E-mail: ipp57@aol.com

Thomas Haller
Telephone: 989-791-4191
Fax: 989-791-4191
Email: thomas@thomashaller.com